SMILE

✢ *The Story of a Face* ✢

SARAH RUHL

SIMON & SCHUSTER

New York   London   Toronto   Sydney   New Delhi

Simon & Schuster
1230 Avenue of the Americas
New York, NY 10020

First Simon & Schuster hardcover edition October 2021

SIMON & SCHUSTER and colophon are registered trademarks of Simon & Schuster, Inc.

For information about special discounts for bulk purchases, please contact Simon & Schuster Special Sales at 1-866-506-1949 or business@simonandschuster.com.

The Simon & Schuster Speakers Bureau can bring authors to your live event. For more information or to book an event, contact the Simon & Schuster Speakers Bureau at 1-866-248-3049 or visit our website at www.simonspeakers.com.

Interior design by Carly Loman

Manufactured in the United States of America

10 9 8 7 6 5 4 3 2 1

Library of Congress Cataloging-in-Publication Data

Names: Ruhl, Sarah, 1974– author.
Title: Smile : the story of a face / Sarah Ruhl.
Description: First Simon & Schuster hardcover edition. | New York :
    Simon & Schuster, 2021. | Includes bibliographical references.
Identifiers: LCCN 2021031063 | ISBN 9781982150945 (hardcover) |
    ISBN 9781982150969 (ebook)
Subjects: LCSH: Ruhl, Sarah, 1974– | Facial paralysis–Biography. | Dramatists,
    American–21st century–Biography. | LCGFT: Autobiographies.
Classification: LCC PS3618.U48 S65 2021 | DDC 812/.6 [B]–dc23
LC record available at https://lccn.loc.gov/2021031063

ISBN 978-1-9821-5094-5
ISBN 978-1-9821-5096-9 (ebook)

*To all the many doctors and healers of every stripe
who have helped me these past ten years.*

*But mostly to the main doctor in my life,
my husband, Tony Charuvastra,
who sees me through, and sees me, every day.*

Considering how common illness is, how tremendous the spiritual change that it brings, how astonishing, when the lights of health go down, the undiscovered countries that are then disclosed . . . it becomes strange indeed that illness has not taken its place with love, battle, jealousy among the prime themes of literature.

—VIRGINIA WOOLF, "ON BEING ILL" (1926)

Sometimes your joy is the source of your smile, but sometimes your smile can be the source of your joy.

—THICH NHAT HANH

Contents

CHAPTER 1

Twins

Ten years ago, my smile walked off my face, and wandered out in the world. This is the story of my asking it to come back. This is a story of how I learned to make my way when my body stopped obeying my heart.

But this story begins with hope—the very particular hope of a birth to come. I was lying down in a dressing gown, cold gel on my belly, waiting as the lab technician looked for a heartbeat. I already had a three-year-old girl, and was expecting my second child. I was also expecting to have a play I'd written to be performed on Broadway in five months, and was slightly nervous about the potential collision of two kinds of abundance.

Suddenly the lab technician pointed to the screen and said, "Do you know what that is?"

"No," I said.

I flashed on the ultrasound I'd had before miscarrying my second pregnancy, when the obstetrician had said the fetus looked not quite right and probably wouldn't last. "Don't, like, go out and get drunk, though," she had said in a tone not quite teasing, "just in case it's viable."

"Uh, not to worry," I had said, wondering what gave her the impression that I would go out and get wasted that weekend.

So this time, I feared the worst as I lay there, nervous, while the lab technician squinted at a screen I could not see. "Look!" she said, pointing. There was movement, a heart beating, it seemed to me. *A heartbeat, that's good*, I thought, but what was wrong? Why was her brow furrowed? Was she alarmed, or, wait, was she pleased? "Did you use fertility treatments?" she asked.

"No," I said.

"Well," she said, "you have twins!"

"Oh!" I said.

"Do twins run in your family?"

"No," I said. My mind raced to keep up with my body.

"You can go to the waiting room," she said. "I'll give you a list of new providers. We can no longer be your ob-gyn because your pregnancy is now considered high-risk."

This was a great deal to absorb—that I had two babies inside me and was also now considered high-risk, so much so that they wanted to get me out of their SoHo office as soon as possible before I got preeclampsia and sued them.

I got dressed. I happened to be alone for this appointment; I had planned to meet my husband afterwards for lunch, where we would celebrate if there was a heartbeat, or commiserate if there was not. Now I was sorry I'd come alone. I wanted to tell my husband, Tony, the news immediately, but it also seemed strange to reveal such big tidings over the phone.

So I texted him: "Meet me at Gramercy Tavern instead of at Rice."

"Twins?" he texted back.

Gramercy Tavern was closed for lunch. Tony and I went to Rice, as planned. We were both in shock; Tony, on top of the shock, evinced buoyancy, elation. Coming from a family of three siblings, he'd always wanted three. Being from a family of two, I'd settled on two. I'd even, at one point, settled on one, when I read in an Alice Walker essay that women writers should only have one child if they hoped to remain writers. "With one child you can move," wrote Walker. "With more than one you're a sitting duck."

At lunch, Tony and I talked about how my miscarried child had wandered back, not to be excluded from this birth. We talked about how we would manage with three. I told Tony my fears: that my body could not contain this much abundance and that I'd never write again. He said he had faith in my body and mind.

At the end of the meal, I got a fortune cookie. I cracked it open. It read: "Deliver what is inside you, and it will save your life."

Everyone seemed jubilant about the news, but I was overwhelmed. I found myself feeling vaguely sick when thumbing through books about multiples in the pregnancy section of the bookstore. There were pictures of breastfeeding triplets, and I didn't want to know about all that. It struck me as grotesque, as though I had once been a woman but was now hurtling towards becoming full mammal, all breasts and logistics. I worried that I wouldn't be able to give enough attention to my three-year-old, Anna. I feared that my body wouldn't tolerate two babies; I feared that my writing wouldn't survive three children.

I called my mother with the news. I gave off a scent of "How can this have happened?"

My mother paused, then said, "Well, your great-aunt Laura had twins."

"Why didn't I know?"

"They were stillborn," she said.

Twins run on the mother's side, skipping a generation. Poor great-aunt Laura, whose heartbreak I never knew. Somewhere in Iowa in the 1950s she buried two babies on the prairie and never spoke of it. I imagined their graves on some grassy plain. I wondered whether Laura gave them names; Laura was dead so I couldn't ask her. The ghosts of my great-aunt Laura's babies would haunt me for the rest of the pregnancy.

When I told friends I was having twins, I was as apt to cry as to laugh. My dear friend Kathleen, a playwright, from a large Irish Catholic family, comforted me, saying, "I love big families. Small families are so boring in comparison." Kathleen had already raised two daughters, and had shown me all the ropes, talking me through potty training and tantrums. Her most comforting phrase was, "I'm sure it's just a stage." At this seismic news she said quite simply, "I'll help you." And I knew she would.

Three months pregnant and terrified, I visited my former playwriting teacher Paula Vogel and her wife, Anne Fausto Sterling, an eminent feminist biologist, on Cape Cod. They said, come, we'll grill fish, we'll take care of you. Paula is the reason I write plays. She has the ferocity of a general in battle, the joy and humor of a street performer, and the tenderness of a mother. That week, she entertained Anna with tissues she made into a puppet. Anna laughed with joy. I was quiet. Paula observed me. "What's wrong?" she asked. She gave me her conjuring, summoning look.

"Will I ever write again?" I asked her.

"Yes, you will," she promised. I looked out at the ocean. This was the same view Paula had shown me years ago, when she'd invited her graduate students out to her Cape Cod home, entreated us to look out the window, and say to ourselves a mantra—*This is what playwriting can buy.*

My first Broadway play was supposed to go into rehearsal that fall; I was not only pregnant, I was extra pregnant. What luck, what abundance. All this bounty, why am I not happy? I thought.

And my mind went back to the fortune cookie: "Deliver what is inside you, and it will save your life."

Did it mean that my life was imperiled, and if I didn't deliver the babies speedily, the pregnancy itself would kill me?

Or did it mean something more metaphysical?

All through the pregnancy I thought, How could my children possibly save my life?

It would take me a decade to find out.

CHAPTER 2

Opening Night

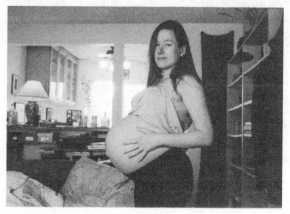

Me, pregnant.

That fall, I sat at rehearsals for my play *In the Next Room, or the vibrator play* at Lincoln Center with my widening belly under the table, watching the actors, and frequently snacking on crackers. I fantasized about the Actors' Equity breaks that come in two-hour intervals, so that I could pee or buy more food. I was the amount of showing where you just look sort of ambiguously fat, not unambiguously pregnant. I wondered if I would even be sitting at a rehearsal table once I had three children under the age of four.

Wearing a strange, green, roomy sweater, I put my arm around a luminous, slender actress for a photograph; she was so small it was as though my arm looped around her waist twice. And I smiled for the cameras.

Nerves are tricky for a playwright the week before any opening, but for Broadway openings, they are nearly impossible. Add being pregnant with twins and feeling like your belly is about to fall through your vagina onto the floor, because your second trimester actually feels like your third trimester, and your third trimester feels like some imagined fourth trimester that can't possibly exist, and what you have is a kind of temporary psychosis.

The week before opening, I was busy doing press interviews. Reporters kept asking me about the nakedness onstage. The play—ostensibly about the history of vibrators—is really about marriage and intimacy. In the play, a woman who has just had a baby is married to a nineteenth-century doctor who treats women with hysteria using the newly minted vibrator, at the dawn of electricity. She begs her husband to treat her, though she herself is not hysterical. At the end of the play, the doctor is naked, in the snow. After the whole play, in which he has barely seen his own wife, he finally sees her, and is seen by her.

I was surprised that the reporters kept asking about the slight bit of male nudity onstage, when the rest of the play treated erotic matters like the orgasm (though under bloomers and sheets). Why the fixation on nudity? I wondered. The journalists told me the nudity felt "in your face" and "endless." I was bewildered. I found the nudity subtle and of short duration. And this is New York City, I thought. Why are journalists shocked by male nudity? Would they have been as shocked by female nudity? Would they even have noticed it? Female nudity onstage often seems like a directorial grace note, whereas male nudity is shocking. We are not used to looking at the male body onstage, and we are definitely not used to looking at male nudity through the eyes of a woman.

* * *

In the last week of previews, for the sake of variety, I sat in the audience on house right for the first time rather than in my usual spot on house left. From this new vantage point, I finally processed the fact that the actor playing Dr. Givings was full-frontally exposed for an impressive five minutes during the leading lady's last soliloquy. Having sat on house left all this time, I'd seen barely the shadow of a male member. But here he was house right in all his glory, distracting the audience during the last moments of the play.

When the leading lady called me to complain that no one was listening to her last monologue because they were mesmerized by the leading man's penis, I thought I had better fix the situation.

The director was recovering from a migraine, so I took it upon myself to raise the issue of the leading man's penis and the sight lines.

I called my beloved leading man, Michael Cerveris, and told him that the leading lady felt upstaged by his penis, and he said, "Unfortunately, my penis is on the same side of my body as my face."

I raced into rehearsal the next day, still intent on helping to adjust penis sight lines, and the stage manager gave me a stern talking-to. He told me to go home and rest. I was incredulous. The ending of my play was at stake, and I should "rest up" until opening night? Yes, he said, rest up.

That week, I waited, napped, and worried.

On opening night, I put on a tentlike navy blue maternity dress with sparkles on the collar. My mother, my mother-in-law, Tony, and I arrived at the Lyceum Theatre, Broadway lights aglow. I squeezed into my seat. The penis sight lines were unchanged, but the leading man was beautiful and honest and unafraid. I got through opening night without drinking a single glass of champagne. Here are Tony and me that night:

At the after-party, we learned that the reviews were good, more than good, really; and the actors were ebullient. We all rejoiced.

The day after opening night, I realized that I was bleeding. From the place you aren't supposed to bleed when you are pregnant. I remembered the couplet I'd written when I'd had a miscarriage earlier in the year, and the melody started to go through my head, a worried mantra:

> *Every month, women practice for this, casual loss as a regular*
> *   thing—*
> *women bleed in private like animals; men bleed in public like*
> *   kings.*

I called my doctor and told him I was bleeding. "Stay home," the doctor said.

"Stay home?" I asked, incredulous. Yes, stay home, he told me. In bed. For the next four months.

CHAPTER 3

Bed Rest

This is a chapter about boredom and entropy. And being forced to stay inside. A chapter in which I plan to finally learn Greek and read all of Marcel Proust in bed but instead I start reading the Twilight series on my iPhone. This is the chapter in which time passes.

I asked my friends to visit and bring books. They cheerfully submitted, bringing bales, boxes, bags of books. All of the books appeared to feature dead twins. *Little Dorrit:* dead twin. I threw it out. A book by Ian McEwan: mention of a dead twin. I threw it out. I wondered about the literary obsession with dead twins and dead mothers.

Sometimes I thought gloomy thoughts about the miscarriage I'd had the year before. I had been at a playdate with Anna, and thought I smelled strange. We had left the playdate and passed several foreheads covered with ash. Ash Wednesday. I remembered how I got home, unloaded groceries, felt a strange pulling sensation, yelled, "Oh!" and went to the bathroom where I saw blood and understood what was happening. Then there was more blood.

Full of grief, I proceeded to watch *30 Rock* as much as possible in order to laugh, and to eat as many Tibetan beef dumplings as possible in order to get my iron levels back up. Eventually, I tried to get pregnant again. I told very few people about the miscarriage. When I did, I found that a large number of women friends had also lost babies. Why didn't we tell each other? I thought. Why did we protect one another from our own grief? Was it superstition? Privacy? Shame?

Now, on bed rest, I knit a crappy little blanket that would never cover even the tiniest baby, let alone two. My daughter's never-failingly normal and cheerful preschool needed a volunteer to cut out hearts for a Valentine's Day project. I was grateful for the task. They sent Anna home with a little packet with scissors and construction paper for me. I cut hearts in bed all day. Pink, purple, magenta—I took out a small scissors and followed the heart-shaped pencil lines the preschool teacher gave me. I was proud of my work.

I felt guilty for not valuing more deeply the free time spent in bed (Don't most busy people fantasize about some time spent in bed?) but the whole concept of time was losing all meaning and value the more I did nothing. Value or time, I thought. If you live in New York City, you might find yourself at the subway ticket machines, in a hurry or in a stupor or both, staring at the words "Add Value" or "Add Time." Before being on bed rest, I had often swiped my MetroCard that read "insufficient funds" and then stood stock-still, staring at those alternatives: Add Value or Add Time.

I have always been confused by these two options, which never fail to glimmer with existential meaning: Do I prefer Value or Time? But isn't time value? Could I not have them both? A subway car often came by while I contemplated this question: value or time, value or time, time or value . . .

And then, invariably, I'd choose value over time because I often lose things and I'm afraid if I buy a month pass (time) I will lose my card. In the end, I am afraid of losing time, so I choose value.

* * *

Oh, what naps I had in those days. The best pregnant nap (which can also be applied to nonpregnant naps) is metaphorically toasting yourself on both sides: I napped on one side for an hour, then flipped, toasting myself on the other side until I was fully slept.

By napping, I cleaved the undifferentiated day into two. Like a ripe avocado cut into two sections, the nap divided the day into what was done and what was still to be done; and with nothing much to be done, it divided the day into the time that passed and the time that would pass. The pit—entropy—was discarded.

The contours of my sleep bled into the contours of the day— far from all the people outside who had business to attend to. Some Americans call a short nap a "power nap" because they think the nap itself must achieve something powerful. These are the same Americans who call a walk a "power walk." What silly terms. Naps and walks may be powerful but their true power is in submission to the moment.

I would have loved to have Rip Van Winkled my way through the entire period of bed rest. I could sleep, grow a beard, wake up, and find myself surrounded by babies. But there were still about ninety days to get through. Time seemed not to move; it seemed to lose all value; but it did, in fact, pass.

That December, I hadn't bled for a while but continued to worry about whether the babies would make it to full term. And whether I would make it with my body and mind intact. If it felt in my second trimester like my belly was about to fall through my vagina, in my third trimester, it felt as though my vagina was about to fall off. That makes no sense, you say. How can emptiness fall out of emptiness? Exactly.

Anna crawled into bed with me and played jumping games. I read the letters of Elizabeth Bishop and Robert Lowell. No dead twins. I loved Bishop's restraint up against Lowell's expansiveness. I adored the borders of their solitude, and how they reached across to find each other. I thought it might make a good play. I read *Twilight.* I tried to bat away loneliness. There was a gulf between what was and what will be that I had all the time in the world to contemplate. A not knowing what I will be. What we will be when we are three . . .

The first snow came. Anna went out with Tony and made snow angels. I watched from the window. They collected snow in a purple bucket and dumped it in a hot bath. They watched it melt.

The idea for bed rest was influenced by the publication of John Hilton's *Rest and Pain* in 1863. He advocated rest for all kinds of maladies: heart attacks, hysteria, ulcers—and pregnancy. Before the nineteenth century, pregnancy wasn't considered a malady. After Hilton's influence, well-to-do pregnant Victorian ladies were regularly put to bed—starting their "confinement" when they began to show.

Half of all women on bed rest get depressed. That number is clear. And women who are placed on bed rest are more likely to have postpartum depression. Although many women have consequences like loss of bone density and muscle atrophy, a fifth of American women are nevertheless prescribed bed rest at some point. The number that is less clear is the one that indicates bed rest as a successful intervention. A 2018 article reported, "Bed rest does not appear to improve the rate of preterm birth, and should not be routinely recommended," and a 2013 study on bed rest reported, "Unnecessary interventions such as bed rest may make the patient (and sometimes the health care provider) feel that all attempts are being made to 'save' the pregnancy." So, though over half of women on bed rest report depression, and though the success rates of bed rest during pregnancy are highly debatable, they still put us to bed.

A Victorian cousin to bed rest was the "rest cure" for women with so-called hysteria. The writer Charlotte Perkins Gilman was prescribed the rest cure, and she drew upon her experience in "The Yellow Wallpaper," published in 1892. In her short story, a woman is put to bed to save her mind from a nervous condition, but goes slowly more crazy from the cure, staring at patterns on the wall from her bed. After a while, it seems to her that the wallpaper appears to move. The woman in bed thinks: "I really have discovered something at last. . . . The front pattern *does* move—and no wonder! The woman behind shakes it!"

One can imagine all the women in the wallpaper standing in for all the women going slowly crazy from a treatment that was surely worse for most women than the diagnosis. The draconian "rest cure" makes the nineteenth-century vibrator cure for hysteria (producing paroxysms in patients) seem delightful. It was thought, at the dawn of electricity, that as many as two-thirds of women could benefit from treatment with a vibrator, which I find hilarious. No doubt two-thirds of women were not hysterical, but they might indeed have benefitted from having orgasms.

Gilman wrote "The Yellow Wallpaper" as an answer to Silas Weir Mitchell, the notable doctor who put Gilman on a rest cure. Mitchell, a neurologist, in his 1877 book *Fat and Blood: And How to Make Them*, theorized that industrial modern life caused people to "live too fast"—and their nerves were damaged as a result. Under his schema, men were told to go West, chop wood, and wrangle cattle; women were told to get in bed, stop reading, and drink milk. For six to eight weeks, these women were isolated from human contact, told not to read or write, and to be spoon-fed while they lay on their backs. They were reduced to the condition of infants.

One of Mitchell's colleagues prescribed the rest cure for Virginia Woolf. Can anyone imagine a more surefire way to make any writer crazy than telling her not to write? And for a writer of Woolf's particular genius, the not-writing and not-reading cure must have been a cruel torture. Woolf writes in *Mrs. Dalloway* of the rest cure, which was prescribed to her character Septimus Smith, who had been traumatized by war: "rest in solitude; silence and rest; rest without friends, without books, without messages; six months' rest; until a man who went in weighing seven stone six comes out weighing twelve."

The rest cure was eventually put to rest when physicians realized it didn't help traumatized veterans of World War II regain their strength; instead, it wreaked havoc on them physically and mentally. Oddly, the same man who invented the rest cure was the father of modern neurology.

Both the rest cure and bed rest for pregnant women were Victorian in origin, and prescribed largely by men, for women. The irony was not lost on me that while my play about hysterical Victorian women was on Broadway, I was in a Victorian stupor at home in bed. I had always been a little Victorian in my fears about pregnancy anyway.

During my first pregnancy, I went to a birth class to "prepare" in Santa Monica, California. We went around in a circle, expectant mothers all, and the facilitator asked what we were most afraid of in the birth process. The women in the birth class looked toned, like they did yoga and had definitely investigated hypnotherapy.

Most of the women said things like: I'm afraid of tearing; I'm afraid of my birth plan going awry; I'm afraid of getting a C-section; I'm afraid of having to get an epidural; I'm afraid I won't be able to bring a scented candle into the birthing center. . . . Then it was my turn. "I'm afraid of dying," I said.

The leader of the group looked startled. And the other women looked away. This was not an answer they heard much, apparently. I thought, Have I read too many Victorian novels or too many newspaper articles about maternal death rates? Had they not read about how maternal death rates in the United States had risen in the past twenty-five years? Most of the women in the room were white. But had they not read that Black women were three to four times more likely to die in this country than white women in childbirth? Did this not horrify them? Shouldn't we all discuss? Shouldn't we be out in the street, protesting?

Didn't these women have friends who had the weirdest shit happen to them after having babies? Like my friend Sherry, a single mother by choice, who suddenly couldn't walk the day after giving birth because she had SPD (symphysis pubis dysfunction)—when your pelvic bone gets thrown out of whack during labor and then you can't walk for a month? (And she happened to live in a sixth-floor walk-up.) Or my friend Claire, who got an embolism in the lung during her pregnancy and got to the ER minutes before dying? Or my friend Alexandra, a professional dancer, who, after giving birth had something called drop foot and one of her feet dragged around limply for months? Or my sister, Kate, who came home from the hospital and her C-section wound opened up and it was green and infected with MRSA, a life-threatening staph infection?

But you aren't supposed to mention any ghastly things to pregnant women. By some tacit agreement, the elders don't tell young women about all the crappy possible outcomes of pregnancy, and they certainly don't mention them to pregnant women.

In any case, the yoga-toned woman running the birth class in Santa Monica changed the subject away from death and we all moved on, to speak of "birth plans," which was, in my mind, an oxymoron.

Also, I feel compelled to reassure you, particularly if you are reading this and pregnant, *All of the above stories have happy endings. Every single one of them.*

From bed, on my second month of bed rest, I wrote letters to the babies.

Dear Babies,

I now know that you are a boy and a girl. The girl is bigger than the boy now, by 12 percent, and you're both over 2 pounds, and the boy is presenting first, head down. I had a dream that the boy came early but the girl stayed inside; and the boy didn't want to breastfeed but instead asked for sausage and cheese, and I was impressed with his verbal abilities. I have been resting up and reading, hoping you stay in there for at least another couple of months. Most people come into the world by themselves, but you will (knock on wood) come into this world together. I hope you both feel safe and sound and cozy there together.

Love,
Mama

Dear Babies,

I was told on Monday that my cervix had effaced to 1.5 cm, so they put me in the hospital to monitor me for contractions. I didn't have too many, so they sent me home and told me to rest even more. You two are kicking away. I am reading, watching movies, and getting

trounced in Scrabble by your father. It is New Year's
Day. I need to go at least 10 more days so that your little
lungs develop, okay? Anna keeps saying, "What do you
think they'll look like?" And she talks to my belly: "What
do you look like?" Then she says, "Well, maybe it's just
best to wait and see when they come." I love you. Keep
baking.

Love,
Your mama

Dear Babies,

I am trying to learn to knit. I am trying to keep busy. You
are wriggling down very low. It's January cold outside. Will
you be Capricorns, Aquariuses, or Pisces? Your sister is
excited to see you. On Monday I will be 32 weeks which
will be a relief, but better to go to 36, don't you think?

Love,
Your mom

I wrote letters to Anna too.

Dear Anna,

You make up absurdist knock-knock jokes. You kiss
my belly for the boy and the girl and you say, "Do you
think they are talking to each other in there? Babies,
are you talking to each other in there?" You say "poop"
and "preoccupied" and laugh hysterically. You go to the
doctor for shots and do not cry. You put lotion on my
legs. You pat my tummy and say you're worried about the

babies squirming in there and you have to protect me.
You are excited about the babies coming and keep asking
when they are coming. You say you will feed them and
dress them and be a good big sister.

Love,
Your mama

When not writing letters, I perpetually searched for the right
book to read, discarding most after reading ten pages. I feared
bleeding, going into premature labor, and losing the babies. I
also feared the self that would inevitably change when they came.

I couldn't venture out of bed to see my play, but I could read
performance reports, written vividly by the stage manager. In
some ways it was frustrating not to be able to see my play; in
another sense, just an extreme logical extension of the position
of the playwright once a play opens. The play opens, and the
playwright is rendered useless, without function. The bodies of
the actors hold the spirit of the play for the audience. There is
nothing more for the playwright to do.

Tony and I decided on names for the twins. For the middle
names, a nod to the ancestors: Patrick for my father, who died
when I was twenty; Elizabeth for Tony's mother. And for the first
names: the intersection where Tony and I met in Providence,
Rhode Island—Williams Street and Hope Street. We would name
the twins William and Hope.

CHAPTER 4

The Itch

Around week twenty-five, I started to itch. The itch started one afternoon in my hands and feet, and spread over my whole body by nightfall. I applied lotion. I put on a humidifier. I scratched. I took Benadryl. I scratched. I rubbed ice on my body. This was not a casual itch. This was the itch of Jean-Paul Marat in his bathtub. (Marat, a French revolutionary, had a mysterious skin disease that caused nonstop itching and open sores, so he spent all of his time in his bathtub, hoping the water would cool the itch. He was murdered in that tub.) I, like Marat, spent a good amount of time in a cold bath, hoping for respite. I took cold baths, even in the middle of the night. As soon as I got out of the bath, I itched. I wrapped myself in cold wet towels. I took off the wet towels. I itched.

When I called my doctor for an explanation, he told me that sometimes pregnant women get itchy. It's normal, he said. "Itch" seemed like a banal description of my experience, so I trolled the Internet, eventually finding a website then called itchymoms.com, where I learned about a condition called cholestasis of the liver, in which bile leaks into your bloodstream, slowly poisoning your blood and causing a terrible itch. More important, it can immediately kill your babies. I was convinced I had the dreaded malady.

I went to see one of the doctors at my practice. He assured me I did not have cholestasis of the liver. "It's very rare," he said.

"But I have all the symptoms," I said.

"How do you know?" he asked.

"Itchymoms.com," I said.

Doctors are not terribly interested, generally, in the online research of anxious patients, or in websites like itchymoms.com, but he said he would do a blood test to reassure me. I waited for the results to come back. Meanwhile, I itched. My husband asked a therapist friend, a brilliant hypnotist, to come do a house call. The hypnotist did a house call and put me in a trance. For a wonderful hour, he convinced me that I did not itch. The hour was up. I itched.

I thought about Great-Aunt Laura and her stillborn babies in Iowa. Cholestasis of the liver can be genetic. It's also more common for twin pregnancies. It only affects one out of a thousand women. The treatment is delivery. I learned that artichokes are helpful for cholestasis. So I ate a great deal of artichokes. I lurched out of bed, boiled artichokes, and dipped the leaves in butter. They were tasty. But I still itched.

A week later, my test came back positive for cholestasis of the liver. Now, rather than seeing the tolerant, kindly faces of doctors indulging their anxious patient, I saw the stern and compassionate faces of brilliant doctors trying to make life-and-death decisions.

"Every three days," they said, "we will do an ultrasound to make sure there is still fetal movement. We cannot promise that in the intervening days the fetuses will not expire." (I couldn't tell if I was imagining that it was at this point they changed their language from "baby" to "fetus.") They made sure I knew that they could make me no promises about the safety of the babies while trying vaguely to reassure me that everything would be all right.

So, from the time I was twenty-six weeks pregnant, every three days my belly and I would struggle into a taxi to the doctor's office to see if the babies had died inside me.

Every three days, the ultrasound technician would rub my belly with gel, move her wand over my belly, her face impassive. My heart would pound until I saw the babies moving on the screen. If they were sleeping, the doctors would tap on my belly to wake them up. Baby B moved more than Baby A. I could feel Baby A's fingers move gently across my belly. Baby B made more global movements. The doctors reminded me that if I stopped feeling the babies moving, I should go straight to labor and delivery.

In bed, I waited for movement in my belly. Movement meant life. Bed rest without news of possible medical calamity is one kind of entropy; bed rest with the anxiety of cholestasis is like being told to do absolutely nothing while your house might be on fire. Thank God there was still one book left in the Twilight series. Plus, the only babies in Twilight are vampires; they're already dead, that is to say—immortal.

I waited for the body parts of the twins to trail across my belly. A hand, a foot. There is something Gothic about that sensation of eight limbs in one belly. Speaking of Gothic, apparently Mary Shelley was pregnant while she wrote *Frankenstein*. Not only that, she had already lost an infant who was born prematurely, leading scholars to later reexamine the tale as a parable of childbirth, and all of its attendant terrors. I had left the land of the Victorian marriage plot and traveled to the land of the Gothic novel.

Two days before thirty-six weeks, my symptoms increased dramatically, and blood tests showed that my bile levels had risen. I called the doctor in the middle of the night, while sitting on the bathroom floor, wrapped in cold wet sheets, in a circle of hell reserved for pregnant women. I was terrified that the increased bile in my bloodstream was poisoning the babies.

The doctor said they would do an amniocentesis the next day to see if the babies' lungs were developed enough to justify early delivery. The next day, Tony and I went into the office, and I lay down on the table, my belly enormous. Tony held my hand, and I watched as a very large needle came towards me. The last thing my tender midsection wanted was a very large needle in it. I looked away as the doctor inserted the long needle into Baby B, my girl. Girls' lungs develop faster than boys'. An amniocentesis at this stage of pregnancy can cause premature labor, and we gingerly went home and waited for the results.

The next morning, the doctors called to say that our baby girl's lungs weren't ready, so our boy's most certainly were not ready. The doctors were walking a razor's edge between the mounting danger of carrying the babies in a poisoned bloodstream and delivering them too prematurely, risking breathing issues and other kinds of trouble. The doctors prescribed me steroid shots, to help the babies' lungs develop more quickly. Tony gave me the steroid shots at home. We waited. I itched.

Two days later, on the eve of thirty-six weeks, my doctor said we'd waited long enough, and told me to go to the hospital. He said there were no beds in labor and delivery and that I should say I couldn't feel any fetal movement in order to get a bed. I longed not to say those words. But I did say them, to get admitted.

When we got there, the doctor said, "How are we delivering these babies?"

"Just take them out," I said.

He said, "I'm happy to do a C-section, but Baby A is positioned head down and Baby B is breech. It's a perfect position for a vaginal delivery, especially since you've already had an almost ten-pound baby." (Anna was a large baby.)

I said, "I think I'm too tired to deliver two babies. I've been on bed rest for three months."

He said, "Just push one out. I promise I'll take care of the other one; I'll pull her out by the legs. Baby A will pave the way."

"Okay, if you say so," I said. I was already starting to look upon this man as my savior, a superhero in scrubs. He even gave us a study to read about the comparative safety of vaginal deliveries for my particular presentation—he was one-part scholar, one-part midwife, one-part surgeon and I relied on him with every ounce of my exhausted body and mind.

I got my epidural. My doctor told me to hug him around the waist to reduce my shaking and increase the chance that the needle found its target. I threw my arms around him, grateful. I got my Pitocin drip. My husband and I watched basketball on television. I never watch basketball. Why were we watching basketball? At midnight time sped up, and they rushed us to the OR. Everyone in scrubs, just in case.

My doctor put on his birthing mix tape. I think it began with "American Woman." Looking into the face of my husband, I pushed William out. I heard a baby cry. "Is he all right? Is he all right?"

"Yes, he's perfect."

Then the doctor reached inside me, as he'd promised, and pulled Hope out by the legs.

"Is she all right?"

"Yes, she's perfect."

The nurses laid Hope and William side by side in a crib and checked them. The nurse told us the babies were holding hands. Before they held the hands of their mother or father, they held each other's hands.

I began shaking. The doctors told me it was time to deliver the placenta. I had forgotten about the placenta. I could not believe that one more item had to come out of my vagina. I delivered the forgotten item. I shook so violently that my teeth chattered. No one ever told me that shaking was normal after delivery, caused by dramatic hormonal fluctuations.

Then the nurses placed both babies on me. And I settled. The shaking stopped. I was wheeled on a gurney into the hallway, where I nursed the babies, one on each breast.

Tony and Anna visit the hospital.

A nurse helped me to my bed for the night. As she rolled me into bed, she saw my nether regions and said, "Oh my God, you're so torn up, you look awful down there." There was more judgment than empathy in her voice, and her touch was rough as she rolled me onto the bed.

I kept trying to feed the babies that night, in between bouts of sleep. Hope, the larger of the two (weighing in at six pounds six ounces), ate greedily, but William was so tiny (at five pounds eleven ounces) that he often just slipped off, or fell asleep while eating.

The next morning, my friend Kathleen brought fresh blueberries to me at the hospital. They tasted like the first and best
food of the world. I was so hungry. I ate handfuls and handfuls. I
felt exhausted, but happy. I looked like this:

CHAPTER 5

Bell's Palsy

The next day, the lactation consultant came in to see how the babies were feeding. My mother was in the corner, holding one baby, while I breastfed the other. The patient lactation consultant tried to teach me how to feed both of them at the same time. There was the football hold . . . that one was tricky . . . and some other hold . . . that I do not remember.

Then the lactation consultant looked at me curiously. "Your eye looks droopy," she said.

Taken aback by the apparent non sequitur and comment on my appearance, I tried a joke, "Yes, my eyes are a little droopy," I acknowledged. "I'm Irish." Most of my ancestors, after one or two gin and tonics, look sleepy, so crinkled and heavy do their crescent eyes become.

"That's not what I mean," she said, kind but firm. "Go look in the mirror."

I got up to look in the mirror in the bathroom. The left half of my face had fallen down. Eyebrow, fallen; eyelid, fallen; lip, fallen, frozen, immovable. A stroke? I was astonished—my face hadn't felt any different before I looked in the mirror. Before looking in the mirror, I was the same person. After looking in the mirror, entirely different.

I tried to move my face. Impossible. Puppet face, strings cut. I came out of the bathroom; my mother saw my face and was alarmed. I called my husband, who is always preternaturally calm (did I mention that he's a doctor?), and told him that I couldn't move the left side of my face. He told me to call the obstetrician immediately and have him call a neurologist. Then he said, "I'll be over in ten minutes."

Tony is a child psychiatrist. He is the sort of person people call in emergencies, the sort of person who neighbors, friends, and strangers tell me brightened their day with the warmth of his regard, or his ability to listen without judgment. Though his voice was calm on the phone, I knew that he thought I may have had a stroke. I am the granddaughter of a doctor, the sister of a doctor, the niece of two doctors, and the wife of a doctor, so I speculate that either I've had a stroke or I have Bell's palsy. I am bad at science but I have differential diagnosis in the blood.

Perhaps more important, my mother once had Bell's palsy when she was in her fifties, so I knew, and she knew, what it looked like.

A neurologist came in, a man I will later grow to despise, but he was a benign enough presence then. He asked me to try to lift my eyebrows. I could lift one but not the other. He asked if I heard a ringing in my left ear. When I said that I did hear ringing, he seemed relieved. He diagnosed Bell's palsy.

Apparently, people who have had a stroke can lift their foreheads fine, but they can't smile or show their teeth; whereas people with Bell's palsy cannot lift their foreheads. A Bell's sufferer might have muffled hearing, hear a tinny sound, or the ear might suddenly not dampen sound, making loud noises unbearable.

I asked the neurologist if the Bell's palsy would go away; and he said sometimes it does and sometimes it doesn't, there is no way of knowing. That was not terribly comforting. But I was relieved not to have had a stroke. The efficient, steroid-prescribing, short-of-stature, short-on-advice doctor left the room.

Tony arrived. All the doctors left. Except for my husband. The twins were in the baby nursery. Outside a blizzard was gathering force. The room was quiet.

That night I cried in the hospital bed with Tony holding me. I wept into his eminently cryable chest. "I'd rather not be ugly for you," I said. I consider my husband a handsome man.

"You never will be," he said.

And he held me.

CHAPTER 6

Sir Charles Bell and the Greeks

Sir Charles Bell, anatomist, artist, and surgeon, provided his name to Bell's palsy in the 1820s. Perhaps he was uniquely situated to diagnose the disease; his observations as a painter allowed him to study human expression deeply. An indifferent surgeon (his amputations on soldiers went horribly wrong most of the time), he contributed significantly to the field of neurology, even developing a theological system based on facial expressions and their relationship to God.

But Bell was not the first doctor to describe paralysis of the seventh cranial nerve. The Greeks, the Romans, and the Persians all noticed a condition whereby the forehead could not wrinkle, the face was paralyzed on one side, and facial spasms occurred. Galen wrote that paralysis affected the "Lips, eyes, skin of forehead, cheeks, and root of tongue." Aulus Cornelius Celsus wrote in the first century: "About the face there originates an affection which the Greeks call 'dog spasm,' and it begins along with acute fever; the mouth is drawn to one side by a peculiar movement."

In contemporary Western medicine there is not a lot you can do to treat Bell's palsy; doctors generally give you some steroids, and then you wait for the nerve to grow back. It's not clear whether Bell's is caused by a virus or by a biomechanical process that compresses the nerve, as with pregnancy. I have since

learned that a very attentive doctor at the onset of illness will automatically prescribe you antivirals (many Bell's cases are caused
by a herpes virus), will also test you for Lyme disease (a large
percentage of Bell's cases particularly in the Northeast are caused
by Lyme), or treat you for Lyme disease as a precaution. This attentive doctor will also give you a script for physical therapy and
tell you to eat plenty of antioxidants. My doctor did none of these
things. Sometimes the nerve grows back completely, sometimes
incompletely, and sometimes it doesn't grow back at all, with or
without treatment; and the doctors don't really know why.

It is mysterious—both the cause and the cure are veiled
in mystery. Doctors don't really know why you get Bell's palsy
(though postpartum women often do), and doctors don't really
know if you will get better—this is what medicine calls an idiopathic disease. Doctors hope that patients will fall into the vast
majority of cases that get better quickly on their own.

The wide range of outcomes can lead to disorientation for the
patient; either I will completely recover in three weeks, I thought,
or I might have paralysis on one side of my face forever.

Was I worried about my husband's reaction to my broken face
because of the male gaze? Maybe. If I had married a woman,
wouldn't I have been concerned with the nature of her gaze
changing with my changing face? Maybe. Medieval love poems
hold that love comes through the eyes, seizing us optically. Aris-
totle thought love passes like an arrow through the eyes and into
the heart.

I said that I found my husband handsome. I still do. His smile
lights up his face, which is round with high cheekbones. His lips
are full and his eyes are brown, compassionate, and alight with
thought. He wears spectacles, and shaves his hair very short,
somewhat like a monk, his widow's peak ending symmetrically

in the middle of his forehead. His mother was Australian and his father Thai, and many ethnicities would be happy to claim him. On any given day he might be thought by a new acquaintance to be Jewish, Latino, Italian, or half Black. A computer program says that the celebrity he most resembles is Laurence Fishburne. When in Thailand, he's less likely to be claimed as Thai and more likely to be thought American. His face is heart shaped like his mother's, and he has his father's penchant for well-tailored suits. Surely my own perception is affected by my love for him—I would say he glows.

Antoine de Saint-Exupéry writes in *The Little Prince*: "Here is my secret. It is very simple. One sees clearly only with the heart. What is essential is invisible to the eye."

But at that time I had little time for romance. I had three children to take care of.

CHAPTER 7

The NICU

Though I was distressed by the fact that my face had fallen down, I looked forward to going home with my babies and seeing Anna, who was being looked after by my mother, and who missed me.

Tony and I began gathering up our things, and I traded a hospital gown for clothes again. Before we left, I gazed at the babies. Hope resembled a white and pink sculpture, her face round and perfect. I looked at William's long fingers; folds of skin hung on his knees, so skinny he was. We affectionately dubbed him Chicken Legs. He was already smiling—I know some would say that's developmentally impossible, but I saw his smile and divined his good sense of humor. His nostrils were so small he had to breathe through his nose and out through his mouth, making a little puff of breath: *pff, pff.*

One of my oldest friends, Andy, a fellow playwright, visited us at the hospital to bring us the car seats we needed to safely transport the babies home. He was the first friend to see my strange new face. I didn't want to show him my face—it felt a little like when a friend comes over and sees that you are still undressed, not ready, wearing your dirty pajamas. But in this case, the dirty pajamas are your face. I also felt bad that he had to come up with something to say. There is no Hallmark card for disfigurement. As in: I'm so sorry your face looks like that now, it doesn't really look that bad, or it only looks bad when you do certain things, or actually I barely notice. . . .

But Andy was reassuring and kind—just as he would have been had I answered the door in my pajamas. We thanked him for the car seats, and Tony and I finished packing our bags to go home.

We started signing our discharge papers and gathered up our things while William was lying in his bassinet. Suddenly, the nurse who was discharging us noticed that William's lips were fast turning blue; he was choking on his own spit-up. The nurse shouted; several other nurses came; and before I could understand what was happening, they were rushing William out the door. "Where are they taking him?"

"To the NICU," said a nurse, running out the door, shouting the shorthand for the neonatal intensive care unit.

I will never forget Tony's face, and his scream, when he saw William's lips turning blue. After the nurses rushed William to the NICU, Tony collapsed on the hospital bed, weeping, worried that it was somehow his fault for not noticing the color of William's lips earlier. He said he should have known—as though the full force of the medical knowledge in his head was colliding with the parenting knowledge in his heart.

Now it was my turn to curl up on the hospital bed and hold Tony; *it's not your fault*, I said, *it's not your fault*.

The doctors put William in a little plastic box and monitored his breathing. And now came the news that the doctors wanted to leave Hope in the nursery overnight under a lamp because her face was yellow with jaundice. I didn't want to leave her there all alone. I asked if I could stay in the hospital with the babies; after all, my face just fell down, and my babies were still there. The doctors said our insurance would not cover an extra night.

I said good night to Hope, leaning over her bassinet, under a heat lamp. I said a prayer to my Catholic God, and I left. I had not said a prayer to a specifically Catholic God in a long time.

CHAPTER 8

A Brief Digression on My Catholic God

When I was thirteen, it was time to enter confirmation class. I'd been baptized a Catholic. At my first Communion, I was so worried I might hold my hands incorrectly to receive the host that, after I received it, I forgot to put it in my mouth. My father shouted from the second row, "Eat it!" So I put the wafer in my mouth. Was that extended moment between receiving and eating the host a harbinger of my spiritual life to come?

In junior high school, Sister Linda was out sick and we had a substitute teacher for Sunday school named Mr. Ivancovitch. He was very tall, and looked a little how I'd imagine Ichabod Crane, with greasy black hair falling over his face and very thick spectacles. The day he took over Sunday school he decided to focus on the bodily suffering of Jesus. He talked at great length and in great detail about how the lungs would have been affected by being on the cross, how the nails would have ripped through the wrists. It made me afraid.

That year, for confirmation we had to go to church every week. I went every Sunday with my father to Saint Francis Xavier Catholic Church, where he was a lector. He was a little tone-deaf, so I could always hear him singing along to the music, his mouth near the microphone, in a kind of monastic monotone.

We had to make our first confession that year to receive confirmation, and I found it odd to have to do confession even if one felt one hadn't really sinned that week. What was worse: to make up a sin or to declare oneself free of sin? To lie or to be prideful? I told the priest I'd been mean to my sister and received penance. Better to exaggerate the meanness in order to get the penance, I figured, than to be so full of hubris as to claim being without sin.

The final confirmation requirement was to memorize the Apostles' Creed and the Nicene Creed. Certain planks of the Nicene Creed troubled me, like, "He is seated at the right hand of the Father." How could we know, I thought, which side he sits on? Also, we had to say that we "believed in one holy Catholic church," but if *Catholic* literally meant "many," why was it that only one church was the real church? I would ask Sister Linda: How can it be loving to look down on other religions, and isn't signing up for "one" holy Catholic church automatically saying other religions are wrong? She dodged my questions. I learned at some point that the Nicene Creed was created and voted upon three hundred years after the death of Christ, unlike the Lord's Prayer, which is recorded in the Gospels. I never had trouble memorizing the Lord's Prayer. But the Nicene Creed . . . my capacity for memorization failed me.

Doubt crept in. I was troubled by the division of labor between nuns and priests. Why couldn't nuns turn wine into blood the way the priests could? Why couldn't Sister Linda talk to God if the Pope could?

I decided I wasn't ready to get confirmed. I told my parents I didn't want to go through with it, and they were philosophical. My mother had abandoned the faith after taking birth control in the 1970s and never went back; she said it felt hypocritical, and she'd rather stay in bed on Sunday morning to read the *New York Times.* But my father still went to church on a weekly basis.

My father told me confirmation was my choice entirely, but I had to go tell Sister Linda in person. So I plucked up my courage and went to her office, which smelled musty and was decorated with pictures of Pope John Paul II. A guitar was in the corner, which Sister Linda played for us from time to time. Terrified, I told Sister Linda that I wasn't ready to get confirmed. I had expected a rain of judgment from Sister Linda, but what I got was mercy, understanding, and gratitude that I had taken the vow so seriously. She smiled gently, told me I could come back to the church anytime, and let me go home.

It turned out I had misjudged the whole situation. It was not the nuns: it was the other thirteen-year-old Americans in my Sunday school class, mostly descended from Irish Catholics, who would judge me.

The day after I dropped out of confirmation class, a small band of Catholic kids circled me on the playground. "What, do you think, you're better than us?"

"No."

"What are you now, Jewish?"

"There are many world religions. . . ."

"So what are you, like, Jewish now?"

"So what if I was?"

"So you're saying we made the wrong choice."

"No, it doesn't have anything to do with you. . . ."

One girl got right up in my face and said, "Jew."

The next day on the front porch, on my gray stucco house with a red door, was a package wrapped in blue tissue paper. A present! I unwrapped it: a plate full of cookies shaped like Stars of David. There was also a Hanukkah coloring book. It was not meant to be a nice present after all. My eyes burned with humiliation. I did not want to tell my mother.

I thought for a while about the time it would have taken my Sunday school compatriots to buy Star of David cookie cutters and bake those cookies. Baking requires effort; it was not an impulsive act of hatred but a planned one. What causes someone to bake hatred into cookies, walk those cookies to someone else's front porch, and cross the threshold, with hate?

My red-haired sister, Kate, was angry and protective. Four years older, she wasn't afraid of anyone. She suggested we prank call the perpetrators. She had a feeling about who it was: most likely my sometimes friends/sometimes tormentors, who lived down the block. My sister left an anonymous message of justice on one girl's answering machine. I never told Sister Linda, or the church, what happened. The matter, it seemed, was settled.

It took me two decades before I would read Thomas Merton and feel an affinity with Catholicism again, a faith that could be rescued from childhood tormentors, a faith that could be combined with other belief systems. But that moment on the porch with the Hanukkah cookies probably shaped whole swaths of my life—the search for an ecumenical faith, the mistrust of institutions, the mistrust of certain kinds of girls.

From that moment onwards, I decided that I didn't want anything to do with the Catholic church. I thought the loving message was not getting through the Sunday school teachers and into the children. The message of scapegoating was getting through instead.

CHAPTER 9

The NICU, Continued

And yet I prayed to my Catholic God to protect my babies. My mother, a lapsed Catholic, said she was now a NICU Catholic.

During the silent taxi ride home from the hospital, I looked out the window, and Tony took hold of my hand. It was horrible to come home without the car seats, without Hope and William. At least I was no longer itchy. At least the babies had come out, safe for now at least.

At home, Anna, three years old and waiting, had made welcome signs. She stamped small letters on a piece of paper: H-O-P-E and W-I-L-L-I-A-M, then carefully water-colored them. This was Anna's prayer for their safe return.

I worried that Anna would hate the twins for turning her mother into a gorgon, that she wouldn't recognize me when I came home. How would I explain that I left the house a smiling pregnant mother and came home with no babies and no smile?

As it turned out, Anna didn't notice the Bell's palsy until later. And when she did notice, she was characteristically sweet. "Your smile is like this, Mama," she would say, imitating a crooked smile. Or, "Good job, Mom, your mouth moved a little bit." When I read to her out loud at night, it was exhausting because it hurt to move my mouth. I lay with her in her trundle bed in the semidark, reading *Fancy Nancy* or *Betsy-Tacy*, working hard at my *p* sounds.

Everyone gave us the advice to sleep a lot while the babies were in the NICU, as though you can store up sleep. But the day after our first night home, the phone rang early in the morning. Ringing phones are not good when your children are in the hospital. I ran to answer, anxious to hear news about William. But this call was about Hope. Hope had a breathing episode in the night, and she had been rushed from the nursery to intensive care.

And so we sped to the NICU in the ice and cold. Once there, I saw William in his little plastic box, breathing. "Where's my daughter?" I asked.

"You mean Baby B?" the nurse replied.

"Yes, Hope."

"She's sicker than your boy, so she's over there."

"Sicker than? What does that mean?" I asked.

"I don't know," she said. "You'll have to ask the doctor when he rounds."

Hope was in a little plastic box, attached to monitors. I wanted to take her out, hold her, and feed her. There was a bottle of formula on top of Hope's plastic box, even though I was breast-feeding. I asked if I could move her closer to William so I could feed them both.

The nurse said, "No. We don't have enough chairs." I spent some time feeling angry at the nurses for not having chairs. And for feeding my babies formula without asking.

I wasn't yet used to my frozen face, and I realized I didn't know how to be ingratiating with strangers without smiling. How does one do that, especially if one is from the Midwest, where a smile is almost a prerequisite for citizenship? They hand them out along with lollipops at the bank. Nice, big, broad untroubled smiles that you have to undo when you move to New York City.

I once read that Americans smile more because we are a heterogeneous country of immigrants, that we don't always speak each other's language, so we smile to signal friendliness to those who are beyond kin. In many nonheterogeneous countries, smiling signals social hierarchy, and it can be taboo to smile at strangers.

In any case, I tried to make friends without smiling in the NICU. I met another mother who had twins the same day I did; she'd had a C-section; her husband wheeled her in a wheelchair to visit her babies.

In the waiting room of the NICU, Orthodox Jewish men prayed. I can still see them now, in prayer shawls, davening. It was the only thing that made all the machines bearable, the human swaying to the internal sound of hope. I wished I could pray in a visible way. I wished I could pray.

It was so cold outside that February. My frozen face matched both the weather and my mood. I took a taxi from Stuyvesant Town, where we lived, up to the hospital twice a day to visit the babies. I fed them, I held them.

Then I went home. I slept. Tony and I came back to the NICU together for the 5 p.m. feeding. Then we ate at the diner around the corner. I ordered meat loaf, a chocolate milkshake, and mashed potatoes, the softest, easiest-to-chew food I could think of with the highest calories for breastfeeding.

The doctor never seemed to be rounding when Tony and I were there, and no one ever fully explained Hope's and William's conditions to us. The nurses gave us very little information, and that made me hate them. The more I hated them, the more food I brought them to eat. The more food I brought them to eat, I reasoned, the more attention they would give my babies—take them out of their boxes, say their names. Though their names were attached to their monitors, the nurses usually referred to them as Baby A and Baby B.

I knew rationally that these nurses' efficiency and brisk professionalism was honed for maximum lifesaving potential. But I longed for them to say my babies' names. The more attention they give my babies, I thought, the more likely it is that my babies will survive. And so I brought the nurses doughnuts and chocolate. And secretly I continued to hate them. Except for one nice nurse, Katie from Iowa, who treated Hope and William as babies with distinct personalities and treated me as their mother rather than as an interloper. At home, every time the phone rang, I jumped.

After three days, the babies were moved to a semiprivate room, again without explanation, and we weren't sure if it was a good or a bad sign. We shared the room with a family called the Rocks.

The Rock babies had been in the NICU for two months, but as far as we could tell, the parents were almost never at the hospital visiting. Katie explained that Mr. Rock had never held the babies. Then one day, Mr. Rock visited. I watched as Mr. Rock held one of his babies for the first time. For two months, he had been too scared to hold his babies because they seemed so fragile.

"Buddy, buddy . . ." he whispered to his baby.

He was so vulnerable, I looked away.

I'd been inside for months, and when I came home from the NICU, the city lights at night felt grotesque and painful, as though they had tongues of fire. Too bright, too much. I'd left the apartment that week to go to only two places—the hospital and to a CPR class recommended for babies who had been in the NICU. I felt as though I should be indoors, or in a dim cave, burrowing, with my frozen face and my babies. Instead the babies were in a too-bright hospital and I was going to a CPR class without them, practicing dutifully on dolls.

In fairy-tale logic, you must trade something for what you desire.

By this logic, I traded my face for my children. And it was a fair trade.

CHAPTER 10

Home

William and Hope.

After the twins spent seven days in the NICU, we were told we could bring Hope and William home. They were so light I could carry them both in their car seats—one on each arm. My mother picked us up from the hospital, driving very slowly on the icy roads.

When we pulled up to our apartment in Stuyvesant Town, Tony and I started to negotiate getting the two car seats out of the back seat, with the tiny babies bundled warmly. An elderly woman knocked on the car door and yelled that we were blocking her way. I felt full of rage—was the rage caused by the steroids I'd been on to mature the twins' lungs?

I yelled right back at that old lady.

* * *

At night, I breastfed one baby to sleep until the other one woke up screaming. Then I breastfed the newly awake baby until the first one woke up screaming. I did this all night long, in a kind of delirium. There was never any fullness or satisfaction. Someone was always hungry. No one was ever full. And their hunger felt like my fault, my responsibility.

I didn't have quite enough milk for both babies, so I supplemented with formula. My lack of adequate milk was possibly because there were two babies to feed, or because they'd been in the NICU, where I couldn't feed on demand and the nurses were bottle-feeding them from day one. Once a week, a lactation consultant followed me around my apartment with a breast pump, telling me to pump when I wasn't feeding, to increase my milk supply. I avoided her.

I had a headache from the Bell's palsy that felt something like a needle had entered my cranium; and loud noises, like children crying, were magnified tenfold. (The seventh cranial nerve also controls a small protective muscle in the middle ear, which normally dampens intense vibrations on the eardrum. Without that muscle, the result is "hyperacusis," or sensitivity to loud sound.) In other words, when the children mewled, it sounded like they were howling. When they howled, it sounded like a heavy metal concert in my brain. At night, when I managed to sleep, I wore an eye patch because I couldn't close my left eye, and the doctor didn't want me to accidentally scratch my cornea.

I still had an ice pack on my nether regions, and Anna insisted on putting an ice pack on her nether regions too. One night I was breastfeeding both babies on the couch; and at three in the morning, Anna snuck out of her room and said, "I want to sit on your lap."

"You can't sit here," I said. "There are two babies there already. Go back to sleep."

"I'm crestfallen!" Anna wailed. (She had learned the word *crestfallen* from the Fancy Nancy books.)

The wise say that love expands to include all children. And the love did expand. The love was boundless. But the lap appeared to be finite.

After my mother went home to Chicago, my mother-in-law came from California to help. A very beautiful woman—not beautiful in a casual way but in a strangers-take-notice kind of way—she entered the apartment full of practical wisdom. It was always a little strange to have such a drop-dead gorgeous mother-in-law, and even stranger when I looked like I'd had a stroke. Elizabeth, or Liz, used to be a midwife in Australia and, as a result, had storehouses of practical knowledge about babies and great compassion for the failures of the body. As a young woman she looked sort of like Grace Kelly, and as an older woman she looked magically not at all old. Maybe her beauty gave her extra empathy for my loss of symmetry.

My mother-in-law was always very close with Tony, her first child. I remember seeing how stricken her face looked when she was to "give him away" to me at our wedding: the terror of giving your son away to another woman who might always be, in some fundamental way, a stranger.

After the wedding, I lured her son, my husband, to New York, towards Forty-Second Street and the theater, away from the desert succulents in California, and away from her. That geographical grief never entirely disappeared, but was much improved by her joy in her grandchildren.

In New York, Liz had a gin and tonic around 5 p.m., we all shared dinner, she put on her slippers, and then she would say to me in her comforting Australian voice, "Now go to sleep, dear." She would stay up all night with the babies, tidying up and drinking strong tea. I would pad out to breastfeed in the middle of the night and we would chat. She would tell me about being a midwife in Australia, about meeting Tony's father, Charlie, in Sydney. Charlie, from Bangkok, came to Australia for medical school; he met Liz in the hospital during his training. But opportunities for Thai doctors in Australia were not exactly abundant, given the White Australia policy that was just about to be dismantled, so Charlie left for Canada.

Liz told me how she followed Charlie to Canada with no money, subsisting sometimes only on bananas. She followed him without knowing how their romance would end—at the time, he was fleeing an arranged marriage to a Thai woman. Liz told me that she worked as a nurse during the day and, at night, taught herself to type by covering her typewriter with bandages so she couldn't see the letters, and banging out all the poetry she could remember. She told me how she was sometimes bored as a young mother and longed to have gone to college. So she bought an eleven-volume set called *The Story of Civilization* and she read those four million words between feedings. Liz loved her dogs, her garden, her children, and her grandchildren, and had little patience for people who were unjust, unkind, or simply stupid. My enemies were her enemies; she took them on. She'd had a cataclysmic divorce from Tony's father and raised three kids mostly by herself, and perhaps as a result was always firmly on the side of independent women. She and I had an easy back-and-forth at three in the morning when most of the house was asleep. There was only the sound of one baby on a bottle she was giving, and the other baby on my breast.

She would tell me that I was a Christian martyr for having a frozen face and breastfeeding twins. We were very close that week. She died a year later of pancreatic cancer.

*   *   *

When my mother-in-law left town, the lack of sleep was still wearing on me. My mother came again, with my sister, for a week. Both heroically stayed up with me—the sleep deprivation when breastfeeding twins can feel like a form of psychosis. Tony moved into Anna's room, and my sister slept in bed with me as we sometimes had when we were little, and we took turns changing diapers all night. When they went back to Chicago I felt bereft.

Anna was still getting up in the night and coming out to find me. It took Tony an hour to put her to sleep every night; on top of feeding and swaddling the twins, Anna would be up again at 3 a.m. Tony was given only a week of paternity leave (it's perhaps worth lingering on that phrase for a moment—*one week* of paternity leave for twins) and then was back to work and needed his sleep. So, my brain addled with sleeplessness—calling a fork a spoon, calling a table a chair, and wanting to go to sleep an hour after I woke up in the morning—I decided to go to a sleep specialist for help with Anna's sleep.

The sleep specialist, a blond skinny woman with bright pink lipstick and an office on the Upper East Side, listened to my troubles, then said, "Every time you cuddle your daughter to sleep, think: I am a bad mother for cuddling with my daughter. I am a bad mother for not teaching her to sleep independently. I am a bad mother for not teaching good sleep hygiene."

Three hundred and fifty dollars later, I was no wiser, no more well slept, and a little more full of rage.

When I did have a moment to sneak out of the house, I went to acupuncture, for the Bell's palsy. The acupuncturist put needles in my face and attached an electronic stimulation machine to the needles. Sometimes the needles gave me bruises, and then I looked like I was battered in addition to looking lopsided.

The acupuncturist told me she cured her father of Bell's palsy in only three days of treatment. This did not happen for me. But within three weeks of treatment with her, I could close my eye manually and it stayed shut while I slept. I still could not blink during the day, but I was grateful that my eye would at least close, so I could forgo wearing a pirate patch at night.

The acupuncturist told me that according to Eastern medicine, Bell's palsy originates in an excess of wind. She advised me to wrap my neck carefully with a scarf when going outside in the wind.

It was very windy out that winter, and frigid. Anna said, "When I am thirsty in the winter, I just drink the wind."

CHAPTER 11

Smile!

Then, out of the blue, good news from the planet of theater, which felt like a distant planet at this point. My play *In the Next Room, or the vibrator play* was nominated for a Tony Award for Best Play. The arrival of this good news, which would normally have felt a little more ecstatic, seemed to reach me at a distance, as though I were now swimming in a different, faraway pool. The Tony Awards *Vanity Fair* photo shoot was the next day. I debated whether or not to go. It will be awful, I thought. They will ask me to smile. But my agent said I should go, so I went.

I was asked to stand on something resembling a red carpet with maybe thirty photographers from different outlets in front of me. I recalled that the poet Elizabeth Bishop once said, "Photographers, insurance salesmen, and funeral directors are the worst forms of life."

I stood in front of the phalanx of strangers with cameras.

"Smile!" they shouted. I tried hard to smile.

"Smile!" they yelled again, peering from behind their cameras. "What's wrong with you—can't you smile for your Tony?"

"Actually, I can't," I said. "My face is paralyzed."

They stared at me, mumbling apologies, and took my picture. I felt sorry, like I was playing a mean joke on them, the one where a kid tells another kid on the playground to ask yet another kid how fast their mother can run, and that child has been prepared to respond: my mother has no legs.

When I was twenty, I studied in England for a year, and for pocket money I worked as a figure drawing model at the Ruskin School of Art in Oxford. Funny that I was less self-conscious dropping my robe—as the imperious painting teacher intoned "Swan!"—than I am smiling for the camera, clothed.

Having my unclothed body interpreted, created by brush-strokes, was far preferable to me than having my features rep-licated, frozen by a camera. When one of the artists asked to photograph me, I said no.

Why is it that people don't generally grin, showing teeth, while they are painted or photographed naked? Is the smile a stand-in for the body's own nakedness, and added to a naked body, too much, a hat on a hat? Children have no compunction about grinning while naked. Is a grin on a naked adult strange because it shows no consciousness of the erotic body?

At any rate, my general impatience and discomfort with being photographed pre-Bell's turned, post-Bell's, to fear and loathing.

I hated the black-and-white photograph that was taken of me that day by *Vanity Fair*. I thought my face looked like water that was going downhill and then stopped, in some kind of deep freeze. I looked existentially pained, though it was taken on what should have been a joyful day. If I had no attachment to my face, I might have thought that the effect was sort of interesting. But appar-ently I did have an attachment to my face, so I thought the effect terrible. The photograph felt somehow taken against my will, just as I felt my smile was taken against my will.

I decided not to be in any more photographs.

Vanity Fair photo.

Of course I was not the first woman to be told by a male stranger to smile. In 2014, the Brooklyn-based artist Tatyana Fazlalizadeh painted a mural called *Stop Telling Women to Smile*, addressing the ubiquity of compulsory smiling in public spaces, particularly for women of color. Women have been told by men to smile from time immemorial.

And my frozen face situation was not the first time men have shouted at me to smile. It was a regular occurrence when I was in my twenties, walking down the street, lost in thought, making up a poem in my head, brow furrowed. A man would say, "What's wrong, baby? Smile!" Or, "Why so worried? Smile!" And I would often just oblige him reflexively, and smile, instead of saying, "I'm thinking, asshole. This is what my face looks like when I think."

And I realized that a man's injunction for a woman to smile as she walks down the street is not an injunction for that woman to experience joy, but for the woman to notice the man walking towards her. The man feels left out of her interior experience— and he feels entitled to tell her what to feel, to describe how she should show her feelings. It is almost impossible for me to imagine walking down the street and telling a man who is a stranger to smile: "Why the worried face? Smile."

I think of Joe Scarborough admonishing Hillary Clinton after a big primary win: "Smile. You just had a big night." And it must be said that compulsory smiling for women is enforced not only by men but also by other women.

The great gymnast Simone Biles, told by a white judge to smile more during a dance competition, famously said, "Smiling doesn't win you gold medals."

It's not lost on me that women of color have an even more historically complicated and deep burden when it comes to compulsory smiling. From the beautiful play *The Immeasurable Want of Light*, by Daaimah Mubashshir: "I smile because that's what people want to see People need to see me smiling Or else it hurts them. It hurts them when they see that I am not happy. . . . Smiling is hard work when you don't mean it. . . . Have you lived your life smiling Have you logged those kinds of miles?. . . My mother . . . is afraid that I will never get anywhere because I let my face rest where it wants to . . ."

What are the perils facing women who rest their faces? Women who are not telegraphing being pleased, being responsive? Can we recognize our own faces at rest, and the faces of other women at rest—our daughters, our sisters, and our mothers?

CHAPTER 12

Actors and Mothers

Three months after the twins were born, I had my first opening of a play with my new face. The play, a three-and-a-half-hour-long epic called *Passion Play*, was performed at an old church in Brooklyn. I loved the performance, but my face did not show signs of pleasure. My mother sat next to me, on my left, and kept peeking over at me, worried. Finally, she whispered, "Are you not pleased?"

"I'm very pleased," I whispered back. "I just can't move my face." My own mother could not read my expression when sitting on my frozen side.

At the curtain call, while photographs were being taken, I retreated to pump milk—two purposes fulfilled at once: avoiding the cameras and relieving the pressure in my milk ducts. I sat by the stained-glass windows in the dark, feeling the very specific relief when milk is unleashed from stony breasts. I had the misfortune of having written too long a play for a breastfeeding mother.

It had taken me twelve years to write *Passion Play*. In that sense, it is both my first play and a more recent play, with about ten plays in between. I started the play when I was twenty-one, when I was living in England, thinking about medieval mystery plays. What would happen, I wondered, if a villager kept getting cast as Pontius Pilate, and had always wanted the role of Christ, played by his handsomer cousin? At the time, I was studying in

Oxford, where stained glass glowed with living history; I walked around the cobblestones that dark winter and medieval literature came to life. It was the year after my father died, and the early darkness of England in November—around four o'clock every afternoon—felt like grief itself.

When I came back from England to Providence for my senior year of college, I approached my playwriting teacher, Paula Vogel, to ask if she'd advise my senior thesis. I told her I wanted to write about representations of the actress in the nineteenth-century novel. Paula said she wouldn't advise that thesis, as interesting as it sounded, but if I were to write a play as my thesis, she would certainly be my adviser. A warm joy crept up in me. *I could write a play. . . .*

It seemed too decadent, too impossibly fun. I said, "Well, I did have this idea, about a guy who wanted to play the role of Christ, played by his cousin. . . ." Paula gave me her characteristic summoning look, a general in battle, a telepathic magician, and said, "Write that play." And so I did. By the end of my senior year I had the first act of what would become a trilogy. And Paula, knowing me to be rather retiring about sharing my work, snuck the first act into the new plays festival at Trinity Repertory Company in Providence, Rhode Island.

On opening night, in 1997, my mother and I were driving towards Trinity, on Hope Street. (What could be more symbolic than the place names in Providence?) Suddenly our car was blindsided on Hope Street by another car driving too fast, and I hit my head and blacked out for a moment. My mother wept—moaning that my father would be so angry with her if she had killed me. "I'm fine," I said. "I only banged my head."

"We should go to the hospital for an MRI," she said.

"No," I said, "we'll be late to my play." And we got to the theater on time, and I saw the first act of *Passion Play* in three dimensions—with massive fish puppets in all their glory—and the audience rose to its feet.

I became a playwright that opening night.

The next day I got an MRI. It was normal. It did not even register the change of vocation.

Sometimes I wonder if, ever since the moment I hit my head on Hope Street, my whole life has been a dream.

And so, there I sat, twelve years later, by a stained-glass window, pumping milk in a Brooklyn church, three kids at home, at the opening night of a now-completed *Passion Play*. The audience was wonderful that night, and the actors were rapturous. I should have felt celebratory—there was Philip Seymour Hoffman, embracing the director; there was the writer Amy Tan in a gorgeous brocade congratulating someone. Normally I would have loved to have met a writer I admired, but tonight I was content to hide. I felt profoundly alone in my face and my body, sitting there pumping milk. Earlier that evening, the director's wife, an actress, told me that she'd had Bell's palsy and it was hell on earth, but assured me that she recovered completely in three months, and I would get better too. I didn't tell her that it had already been three months. I felt inside a paradox: I thought I could not truly reenter the world until I could smile again; and yet, how could I be happy enough to smile again when I couldn't reenter the world?

If my own mother could not deduce what I was feeling from my frozen face, how could a stranger possibly know what emotion I was trying to project? My mother said she felt guilty for not knowing what I was feeling; she'd even had practice with Bell's palsy; she'd experienced it herself.

My mother became aware of her Bell's palsy when she started drooling while eating popcorn in a parked car in Illinois. Not long after, she came to my graduation in Rhode Island, with her speech slurred, a drooping eye, and in pain. My mother was a formidable woman, an English teacher with a PhD, and a gifted actress; she was now a recent widow and seemed fragile, unsteady, traveling without my father. And she had to meet new people without being able to smile at them and with her speech compromised. My mom is excellent at meeting new people. She could get the life story out of a post. She is an inveterate question asker, has boundless curiosity about the world around her, and always has at least seven probing questions at the ready to be fired off. But she didn't ask many questions on that trip. Her asymmetrical face with its half smile seemed like a marker of grief—a metaphor for the strange asymmetry that comes after twenty years of a marriage, suddenly alone. Two becomes one, prime asymmetrical number.

Her face cleared up quickly after that trip, though. She would act in many more plays, hitting her stride in her seventies after retiring from teaching, and acting in as many as three shows a year in Chicago. I asked her once if she was terrified when she got Bell's palsy because of her acting life. She thought about it for a moment and said no. She said the vanity part was not what she loved about acting. She said she never looked in the mirror before going on. "You don't like being looked at?" I asked.

"No," she said. "The makeup and the costumes are a trial. What I love is language and an audience to tell it to."

I was intrigued by my mother's professed lack of vanity when she had Bell's palsy. Was I raised not to be vain? My mother is an actress but never plucks her eyebrows. They continue to grow, sprawling upwards and outwards. "They make me look distinguished," she said, "like my grandfather." My mother always said she wanted to be a "character." She would walk down the staircase during my childhood, reciting the maid's speech from Ionesco's

Bald Soprano. That speech is, in its own way, about asymmetry. My mother would proclaim triumphantly, in a cockney accent: " 'Donald's daughter has one white eye and one red eye like Elizabeth's daughter. Whereas Donald's child has a white right eye and a red left eye, Elizabeth's child has a red right eye and a white left eye! . . . My real name is Sherlock Holmes.' " My mother's improvisational boldness gave me the sense that the world could be a happy place, if only you were willing to be silly.

My mother's desire to be a character merged with reality at some point. Ever my protector, she once yelled at a critic who had disliked one of my plays. The critic in Chicago was on a blind date at a café when my mother spied her. "You savaged my daughter," my mother said. "That's not the function of criticism."

"And I do think it's the function of criticism," said the woman critic.

Critics, beware my mother. She might yell at you on a blind date.

From almost before I can remember speaking, I remember being in the dark of the theater watching my mother act. Before I could write, I would dictate notes to her about the plays she was in, and she would pass them along to the director. As a child, I watched my mother play heightened characters onstage from the Nurse in *Romeo and Juliet* to a character from a Flemish painting in Caryl Churchill's *Top Girls*, screaming gorgeously about potatoes and what comes out of the devil's bum. I have watched my mother die onstage, find the dead bodies of others onstage, and keen; and I have seen her sing a Bruce Springsteen song while holding a broom for a microphone. I have always been used to watching my mother transform. With her short red hair, rich voice, and her sense of the absurd, she's an intensely expressive rather than a vain actress.

My father used to allude to what he called my mother's "quick and darting mind." My father's mantra was that we girls must marry our intellectual equals, a mantra I wish more fathers would tell their daughters, and onstage my mother valued her intelligence over her image.

But beyond vanity, was she not worried about making adequate social facial expressions when she got Bell's palsy? I asked her, and my mom said she didn't worry about that. Once she realized that Bell's palsy not only wouldn't kill her but also wasn't her fault, she stopped worrying. My mother has struggled with her weight since her thirties, and was often told by her father, a doctor, that being overweight would cause her terrible medical issues. Perhaps as a result, the feeling of being at fault for any medical problem has always plagued her.

When she got the diagnosis of Bell's palsy, she asked the doctor, "Is it my fault because I'm fat?"

He looked at her, quizzical. "No, of course not," he said. "Why would you think that?"

"Because I always think my medical issues are my fault because I'm fat."

"Well, this is definitely not your fault," he assured her.

She said that she was then relieved, though she did take to her bed, and refused to go out.

One evening, during her isolation, she watched a documentary called *Dwarfs: Not a Fairy Tale* on HBO, called me, and cried, "Those brave dwarves!" (I said I wondered if the preferred term was now "Little People.") "Going through the world so bravely and not being able to hide! They give me hope about my face." After that, she got out of bed and showed her face to the world again. The empathic power of art shifted my mother's consciousness about her changing face.

The fact that my mother didn't worry overly about expressiveness made me wonder if she had a more mobile face during her bout than I had. My mother had a pronounced droop, I remember, but not a frozen face. Apparently, if you have zero movement in your face with Bell's palsy, it's a marker of how severely the nerve was damaged. Complete immobility (which is what I had) is indicative of more serious damage, and the possibility of never recovering.

After my mother's two-month retreat from the world, her face got much better.

It's hard to know where my mother ends and I begin. Isn't that the story with so many mothers and daughters? I remember when I was little she taught me what a Venn diagram was. We were on a train, from Chicago to Texas, to see my cousins. In the dining car, on a napkin, my mother carefully drew two circles, showing me the overlapping section. "What do these two circles have in common? Here . . ." she said, pointing. I was fascinated by the logic of that diagram.

Mothers and daughters: two circles, and the all-important bounded sections where they are complete unto themselves. Daughters perhaps have a tendency to point at the differences, mothers to point at the commonalities.

My mother and I both love theater, both love books, both were afflicted by Bell's palsy. And also, the bounded section— where two are not alike—she recovered.

CHAPTER 13

The Duchenne

Me in my backyard, 1979.

A t night, I dreamed that I could smile. The smile felt effort-less in my dreams, the way it did in my childhood.

Then I would wake up and look in the mirror: the same frozen grown-up I was the day before.

After three months, my face still didn't appear to be getting any better, and at my actress friend's advice, I went to her physical therapist at a high-end gym. (I don't go to high-end gyms.) The physical therapist greeted me with, "You look good for someone with Bell's palsy." I blanched. He went on: "I mean, you should see some of my clients with Bell's palsy!" He massaged my neck a little and asked me to move my face in ways that I couldn't possibly while I looked at myself in the mirror. He told me to come back in a week.

The following week, I went back to the physical therapist at the fancy gym. He asked me, "How do you think your face looks this week?" The bid for self-assessment caught me off guard.

"Uh . . . a little better, I think?" I said.

"Really?" he said. "The whole left side of your face looks totally enervated."

"Oh," I said.

"Try to open your mouth," he said. I tried to open my mouth wide, but it just drifted oddly to the side. "Try to blink," he said. I could not blink at all on the left side.

I found it humiliating to look in the mirror and be unable to perform simple tasks in front of the small audience at the gym. A friend of the physical therapist walked by and saw me making bizarrely contorted faces in the mirror. The friend said, "Dude, that's crazy!" Then he laughed, and took a picture of me, without my permission, with his iPhone. I probably looked a little like Donald O'Connor's iconic Cosmo from one of my favorite movies, *Singin' in the Rain,* in the scene where he made amazingly strange faces while singing "Make 'Em Laugh." But I was making faces without the intent to entertain.

The physical therapist apologized for his friend, but the photo made me feel violated, and I vowed never to return. And I didn't.

As for what I sounded like, I couldn't say my *p*'s because I couldn't close my mouth completely on both sides. This was particularly unfortunate when I tried to say my daughter Hope's name.

I remember one conversation I had with a stranger at a loud bar in the East Village after a theater opening. The polite stranger asked, "So, what are your twins named?"

I said, "William and Ho—"

"Excuse me, I don't think I heard you right. William and—Ho?"

"Ho—pe," I said, sounding like I'd had a stroke.

"Ho?"

I spelled and yelled, "H-O-P-E! Like the feeling?"

"Oh, Hope!"

"Yes!" I yelled, wishing I could smile at the absurdity of the situation (that's right, I named my twin babies ho and William). Instead, I just nodded.

I never specifically prized my smile, but now I realized I used to have a rather nice one. Symmetrical and full. I began to feel what a loss it was not to be able to smile at strangers to indicate permission to speak, affinity, or understanding. I realized how we count on that subtle coding at least a hundred times a day.

I remember, shortly after September 11, running into a woman I knew vaguely at a cocktail party. We discussed the vagaries of travel and she said, "I always smile at potential terrorists on airplanes. I figure if they smile back, they are not terrorists. And if they don't smile at me, but I give them a nice big friendly smile, I think maybe they'll decide not to blow up the plane, because they've made a connection with a stranger."

"How do you know who to smile at?" I asked.

"If their beards are long enough that they appear to be in love with God."

"What's wrong with being in love with God?"

"Well, if a person seems to be in love with God, but in an angry way."

"Oh," I said, thinking that her brand of racial profiling was eccentric. "How many lives do you think you've saved by smiling at potential terrorists?"

"Thousands," she said, and smiled broadly, with her beautiful bright red lipstick and a flash of white teeth. And then she was gone.

I thought of all the planes I have not saved by not smiling at strangers but that were saved anyway, by the passengers' own common humanity.

I recently came upon a picture of myself smiling broadly in my high school yearbook. The lipstick I am wearing is Revlon's Toast of New York, a shade my friends and I found at an Illinois Walgreens and wore all the time, feeling grown-up. It was dark red, tinged with what I imagined was the color of brown toast, thus, I thought, the word "Toast." My Midwestern mind was literal even about lipstick, apparently.

In the photograph, I smile with teeth, sporting bangs, my head tilted a little to the side. The photographers told all the girls to tilt their heads and smile; whereas the boys were less likely to smile with teeth, and looked at the camera directly. The girls, whether they knew it or not, were trying to produce Duchenne smiles, and the tilt of the head, in evolutionary terms, indicates submission.

High school yearbook,
Duchenne smile.

The Duchenne smile is named after Guillaume Duchenne, who studied facial expressions by mapping the faces of inmates at mental hospitals in the nineteenth century. The Duchenne indicates a smile echoed by the eyes crinkling in response—the gold standard for a smile evincing authentic enjoyment: grace, over and above the will.

Duchenne described the difference between voluntary and involuntary smiles this way: "The first obeys the will but the second is only put into play by the sweet emotions of the soul." He called the muscle that creates movement in the eyes during this smile the "muscle of kindness."

One year in high school I decided to smile at everyone I passed in the hallway between classes as an experiment to see if they smiled back. They almost always did. This pleased me.

My very first week in New York City, in my early twenties, I smiled at a man sitting across from me on the subway who took it as an invitation to come sit next to me. He then put his other earbud from his headset over my ear, saying I had to listen to a song. I obliged, my head tilted towards him. Once I smiled at him, I felt it was too late to say no; my smile had given permission. I remember an old woman across from me, looking at me, shaking her head.

There is a complex set of unspoken rules guiding women's smiles in public. Whether and how long she smiles . . . at night . . . during the day . . . at strangers . . . in new neighborhoods . . . on her own block . . . in boardrooms . . . in banks . . . her smile can be protective, a talisman, something to withhold or bestow.

Without my smile, I began to develop odd ways of signaling approval or friendliness. I vocalized more. I made weird gestures with my hands upon seeing people I liked, unable to smile naturally upon recognition. Laughing without smiling was a predicament. I could make a chuckling sound, but found it difficult to feel the spontaneous sensation of belly laughing without being able to fully open my mouth.

I was busy finding ways to signal my internal life to my family and friends, who knew me before (and in my mind I was starting to draw a thin line separating the me from before and after), but it was harder to negotiate meeting people for the first time. Strangers did not have an earlier template of my self and intentions to graft my new face onto. And so when I met new people, I internally debated: Do I explain that I'm recovering from facial paralysis so may seem unfriendly or disinterested? Or do I just make slightly forced gestures with my hands to communicate interest and excitement because I can't raise my eyebrows? I split the difference. Sometimes I explained myself; sometimes I just made weird little waves to communicate friendliness to other parents at the playground and said "oh" a lot to show interest. I felt like an overenthusiastic and clumsy American tourist who didn't know the language of the country she was visiting.

I had lunch with my actress friend, who is probably objectively one of the most expressive people alive in the world, and who visited right after the twins were born; and it seemed particularly odd not to be able to mirror her facial expressions at all. I found myself making odd cooing noises while she told me stories, moving her extremely mobile face.

If a person had a smile that was incredibly beautiful and frequently aimed at me, it was a kind of social torture. I tried to return the smile, but through some tragedy of symmetry, a half smile can look, in fact, like a grimace. Better not to make any expression at all, I thought. Better to say *mm* . . . *hmm* more and keep my face impassive.

Some say that for many mothers the postpartum fog or dip is greatly relieved by seeing the baby's first "social smile." I did love seeing all my babies smile. William's smile had a sense of mischief from the time he was newborn; Hope had a calm self-possessed smile; Anna had a smile as though we were sharing a secret.

Not being able to smile fully back at my babies became a kind of obsession.

I wanted to smile at my babies most of all.

CHAPTER 14

Still Face and the Tony Awards

If you are ever worried about the effect your affect has on your baby, do not watch videos online of mothers making what psychologists call "still face" to their babies. In these experiments, mothers look with a face devoid of expression at their babies, then their babies freak out. These videos were made by psychologists trying to study the effects of cold or depressed mothers on their offspring. The effect of the still face on children, these psychologists proved, is, in a word, bad.

I watched these videos and thought: Oh dear, am I looking at my babies with still face? And I wondered: What effect will it have on my babies that I can't smile at them? Will they feel unloved? Will they have crooked smiles because they are imitating me? How will they know I love them unconditionally, that I delight in them?

My husband, the psychiatrist, said, no, you haven't looked at them with still face. They can see that one half of your face is smiling. But still I wondered: Can babies read the warmth of intention from a thwarted smile? Aren't they in the middle of learning how the face is coded?

One afternoon that spring, alone with the twins, I walked them outside in their double stroller, and sat on a bench under the

flowering trees in Stuyvesant Town. Hope mewled, hungry.
I took her out of the stroller and nursed her. Then William
woke up, wanting to eat. I put Hope down and put William
on my breast. Then Hope started crying like her heart would
break. Feeling helpless, I put both of them back in the stroller
and wheeled them back towards our apartment so I could feed
them at the same time in bed using the football hold. The
twins screamed in their stroller, their faces red. By the time I
got home, and got them positioned on the bed with pillows,
Hope kept crying and crying, refusing to eat, while I fed William. I lay in bed despairing; one baby crying, the other baby
eating.

Time that spring was a blur of milk and tears; the veil between
night and day pierced. I couldn't write. I lost a lot of weight.
Oh, well, it's stress, I thought. And breastfeeding. My internist
screened me for stress, giving me a worksheet. I checked off the
things that caused me stress. It turns out that my children were
causing me stress. I handed back the worksheet.

"It looks like you are experiencing stress," she said.

"Yes," I said.

"Is there any way you can avoid the source of your stress?" she
asked, frowning at the worksheet.

"You mean avoid my three children? No, not really," I said.

But joy? Of course there was joy. Amid the stress and the sleepless
nights, there was plenty of joy.

And yet, when I look back at those years, there are no pictures of me smiling with my babies. And in this day and age, we
sometimes seem to care more about the record of joy than the
experience of joy itself.

*   *   *

After I had Anna, I had more or less figured out how to write again. I placed my desk in her nursery and wrote while she napped. When she started walking, I put a toddler gate between her side of the room and my side. I brought her to rehearsals and breastfed her in the dressing room. I took her with me out of town for premieres.

With Anna, I had religiously followed the dictates of "attachment parenting"—wear the baby, bring the baby to work, feed the baby on demand, sleep with the baby. When I was at rehearsal, I requested a green room so I could nurse on rehearsal breaks. (I know of no theater that has a dedicated nursing room yet.) I even became emboldened enough to ask a theater for a babysitter's train fare when I worked out of town. Mostly when I asked for accommodations like a dedicated nursing room or a train ticket, I was given them, sometimes with the admonishment not to think of it as precedent setting. But now that I had three children, I mostly stopped asking for accommodations. My brood seemed so utterly antithetical to how the American theater was set up for its workers that I simply did my best to go about my business. And in the back of my mind, I thought: it's my own fault that the contours of my family are antithetical to this profession—so I better make it work and cover up the chaos. It did not occur to me then that the profession must also shift to accommodate its workers.

In the attachment parenting books, when you look up twins in the index, there's very little information. The books mostly say: gee, hope you don't work (I did work) and hope you have a fully committed partner (I did). With the advent of three children, the dividing line between nursery and desk became too porous. I couldn't bring two babies to rehearsal to breastfeed; it was too distracting. To keep up my milk supply, I alternated bringing Hope or William with me to rehearsals of my adaptation of Vir-

ginia Woolf's *Orlando* (an epic tale about a man who suddenly
changes gender throughout the ages). The costume designer
didn't realize I had twins, and thought I was making a political
point about the play, by dressing my baby first as a girl one day,
then as a boy the next.

"No!" I said. "There are two of them!"

While I breastfed Hope or William at rehearsals, the other
two children were at home with our wonderful caregiver, Yangzom. We met Yangzom when Anna was a baby and she seemed
heaven-sent. Patient, calm, kind, she was better at getting Anna
to sleep than I was. I had resisted having any more care than I
absolutely needed when Anna was a baby, for both economic and
emotional reasons, but now that I had three children, Yangzom
and I were officially a team. I would breastfeed one baby while
she bottle-fed the other. I would take Anna to a doctor's appointment while she took the twins on a walk.

Yangzom came to this country from Tibet, and is a devout
Buddhist. Little did I know that as time passed, she would also
become my teacher.

When Hope and William were three months old, I was invited to
an awards ceremony for women in theater; I thought it would be
a casual affair (probably because it was for women). So I brought
Hope along rather than a breast pump; the company seemed
more jolly and we mingled in the lobby. I held Hope swaddled
to my chest.

Suddenly there was a great movement to gather all the award
recipients onstage, where we were to be seated behind the formidable lineup of speakers. Good God, I thought. I had no idea
we'd be *visible*. (Funny that I had such an assumption about an
awards ceremony for women; instead, at the joyful Lilly Awards,
it was all about visibility.) So there I sat onstage with baby Hope

on my lap. She was quiet during the first half of the ceremony, which, as it turns out, was long. But then Gloria Steinem started to speak (be still my heart, Gloria Steinem), and Hope began to cry. I looked to my right, panicked, where the writer Mary Rodgers smiled at me, comforting; and in an act of maternal telepathy, she nodded with approval as I took out my breast to nurse, three hundred people watching in the audience. Hope quieted down. Mary Rodgers, whose book *Freaky Friday* I had loved as a child, patted me on the leg and said, "That's right, that's the way to do it."

Later that month, I realized, frazzled, that I needed something suitable to wear to the Tony Awards. Fashion houses sometimes volunteer to dress the actors and actresses nominated for Tonys, but they seemed to have no interest in dressing a harried playwright/mother of small children. I ran into Bloomingdale's on a break from nursing, and snatched the first blue gown that fit me. I feared it looked a little like a prom dress for a grown-up lady, but it fit, was not overly expensive, and I have always loved the color blue.

I knew a social-worker-turned-makeup-artist and asked her for help before the Tonys. She said that as a social worker, she once did makeup for victims of domestic violence, and found that she could make a woman feel better by giving her a makeover and covering the bruises. So she changed careers. She was very gentle as she applied my makeup. I told her that I couldn't blink, so to be careful with the mascara wand, which came at me, looking large and dangerous.

At the awards ceremony, I walked down the dreaded red carpet. When asked to smile, I turned up the right side of my lips ever so slightly in order to avoid asymmetry. I figured there was so much Botox around that perhaps my unmoving forehead might be fairly unnoticeable.

I fleetingly thought: but Botox creates a paralysis that is symmetrical and is therefore beautiful; Bell's palsy creates a paralysis that is asymmetrical and therefore unpleasant.

I went to the bathroom to pump breast milk at a commercial break. After pumping, I realized in a panic that I couldn't zip myself back up. I looked around the bathroom, my gown at half-mast, Broadway luminaries flushing all around me. Sweating, I looked around the ladies' room and hitched up the back of my dress with my right hand, my left hand holding my black pump kit that looked a little like a bomb. I caught the eye of a notable set designer, also a mother. I asked her if she'd zip me up, and she laughed, and happily obliged.

I got back to my seat and watched the dancers in the show flash their legs and smiles, making me think of scissors. The teeth, whitened. The bags under the eyes, diminished by cream intended for hemorrhoids. Show business, in all of its glory, is not really for the unsmiling. These actors with their décolletage and their light-catching smiles seemed like superhuman avatars for all the rest of us in the dark—the imperfect, the clumsy, the asymmetrical.

There was no real danger that the television would show my face during the awards anyway. I didn't expect to win, as my play had already closed, and they barely ever show the playwright on TV. My play didn't win, but I got a nice bag of swag, which I kept for Anna. I almost touched Cate Blanchett's shoulder at the after-party. And I went home.

Whether you win or you lose, you get to go home, and how that homecoming feels in your body is more predictive of one's happiness than winning or losing. Mainly, I felt tired.

Once we got home, Yangzom told me she had hoped I would win so that I would be able to thank people on television. As a Tibetan

Buddhist, Yangzom is always attuned to values like gratitude. I've always thought it was a strange quirk of awards programs—that they foster greed and the desire in artists to win, mainly so that artists can express gratitude in public. The system creates competition among people who are otherwise compatriots, so that the winners can say publicly that they're grateful to their third-grade teacher, their mother, their children, God.

In truth, we don't have to win to be grateful. We can always thank the people we love, the people who help us, even when we don't win an award. We often just forget to.

At any rate, I thanked Yangzom, and she went home.

CHAPTER 15

The Mona Lisa *and Illness as Metaphor*

Mona Lisa

I t used to be people didn't smile for pictures. It was unseemly to do so. Those men in suits and women in corsets looked straight ahead. American presidents didn't smile with teeth for photographs until the daring and charismatic JFK. It's much easier to smile for a camera than to smile for a painted portrait, for which you must pose for hours, usually with a solemn face. The *Mona Lisa* was unusual in its time partly because smiling portraits were abnormal. And then the ambiguity of her expression, the secret that it contained: Was she genuinely happy, or a little sad? If you walk around the painting, her expression seems to change slightly, affected by peripheral vision and distance.

Leonardo da Vinci's contemporary Vasari wrote, "While painting her portrait, [Leonardo] employed people to play and sing for her, and jesters to keep her merry, to put an end to the melancholy that painters often succeed in giving to their portraits." While Leonardo made his live model merry by day, he went to the morgue by night, peeling skin off cadavers and studying how muscles created facial expressions. Some have called the *Mona Lisa* "the uncatchable smile" because of the ambiguity of her expression. Does she look sadder up close, but happier at a distance, like many people we know?

Neurologists have studied her smile, calling it slightly asymmetrical, expressing happiness only on one side, the left side, thus more likely to be interpreted as a lie. In one study, forty-two viewers were asked which of six basic emotions were expressed by the left and right sides of the *Mona Lisa*'s smile. Almost all said that the left half of the smile evinced happiness while the right side was interpreted variously as neutral, disgusted, or sad.

Because the *Mona Lisa*'s eyes and forehead are not engaged in her smile, it's often thought not to be genuine, spontaneous, like the Duchenne smile. And if she exhibits an "unfelt smile"— what is she hiding? A pregnancy, as some have suggested? That she is actually a man or a self-portrait of the artist? A prostitute? A memory of the artist's mother (from Freud)? A hidden code (from Dan Brown)?

What is she thinking, *what is she thinking*? This question of the *Mona Lisa*'s interiority has obsessed viewers and art historians, perhaps because of the complexity of her gaze, the relationship between surface and depth.

Long ago, when I visited Thailand to meet Tony's extended family, one of his relatives kept calling me Mona Lisa. Was it because I tended to smile with my mouth shut? Or was I not forth-

coming? What secrets did I have to hide, after all? This was long
before having Bell's palsy.

What am I not telling?

I am a person of little vanity. Or so I thought until I couldn't
move one side of my face. When I first read Charlotte Brontë's
Villette twenty-five years ago, I identified with Lucy Snowe, the
narrator. Not terribly noticeable one way or another. Lucy Snowe
opines:

"No mockery in this world ever sounds to me so hollow as that
of being told to *cultivate* happiness. What does such advice mean?
Happiness is not a potato, to be planted in mould, and tilled with
manure. Happiness is a glory shining far down upon us. . . ."

Not actively trying to be happy, Lucy Snowe travels from England to a small town in France, Villette, to be a governess (just
as Charlotte Brontë once traveled to Brussels to be a governess).
Isolated by temperament and language, Lucy Snowe retreats into
her mind. This is Brontë's first and last novel—first because she
based it on an early manuscript, last because she finished it just
before she died.

Unlike Victorian novels whose heroines are foot forward and
on the search for a husband, *Villette* is more interested in the
quiet, interior life of its narrator. No one seems to love *Villette*
as much as they love *Jane Eyre*, but I love it even more for revealing this strange ghostly interior. From the time I started writing
plays, I was interested in how to make the small, quiet moments
theatrical—the kind of moments that appear more frequently in
a poem or a short story. How could the theater, I wondered—this
external, swashbuckling, embodied form—reveal the quiet?

In *Villette*, there are few Gothic theatrics. The narrator seems
to be invisible. She disappears more and more, even though she

is controlling the narration, the consummate observer. At the end of the novel, she finally makes herself known. It is astonishing.

How to experience joy when you cannot physically express it? I perseverated on this question. And I despised myself for what veered dangerously close to self-pity. I had three healthy children, and an irritating chronic condition that did not threaten my life. I felt joyless, then guilty, then angry. I often try to solve problems by buying books.

And so I bought a Buddhist book about anger—called *Anger*. In this book, the wise and compassionate Buddhist monk Thich Nhat Hanh details a meditation on anger in which one should breathe, then smile with love. The idea is that physically producing the smile creates the sensation of peace during meditation. This is not unlike the neurological finding that expression produces emotion rather than the other way around. It's also not unlike Charles Darwin's suggestion that "the free expression by outward signs of an emotion intensifies it. On the other hand, the repression . . . of all outward signs softens our emotions." But Buddhists figured out this emotional technology centuries ago.

So I tried. I sat. I meditated. I attempted to smile while meditating. But I was painfully aware that my half-smile grimace was not approximating the right feeling. My face felt like a poorly made puppet.

Thich Nhat Hanh's book counseled: "You know what to do to look more beautiful. You don't need any cosmetics. You need only to breathe peacefully, calmly, and smile mindfully."

I breathed calmly, then thought: But what if I can't fucking smile?

I read on: "If you can do that one or two times, you will look much better. Just look in the mirror, breathing in calmly, breathing out smiling, and you will feel relief."

The idea of looking in the mirror while smiling was the last thing in the world that would have given me any relief. I wanted to throw the book against the wall.

And yet I love Thich Nhat Hanh. In another of his books, he writes:

> When I see someone smile, I know immediately that he or she is dwelling in awareness. . . .
>
> A friend wrote this poem:
>
> I have lost my smile.
> but don't worry.
> The dandelion has it.

Screw that dandelion, I think. I want my smile back.

I was full of self-blame for my face not getting better. (The repeated thought patterns went like this: It's my fault for not sleeping more; it's my fault for not being happier; it's my fault for having two babies; it's my fault for not having a C-section; it's my fault for not going to acupuncture right away; it's my fault, it's my fault. . . .)

Susan Sontag argues, in *Illness as Metaphor,* that the overuse of metaphor for disease often ends up blaming the victim. She writes: "Illness is *not* a metaphor, and . . . the most truthful way of regarding illness—and the healthiest way of being ill—is one most purified of, most resistant to, metaphoric thinking."

The difficulty is that one wants to give one's illness meaning, just as one wants to give one's suffering meaning. But if you give your illness too much meaning, you become the agent of your own decline. I have known far too many women who are apt to blame themselves for things large and small, medical and non-

medical. Are writers in particular apt to look for symbolic meaning rather than for answers rooted in biology? Had I begun to
create an untenable, unsustainable internal metaphor for my
physical inability to smile?

Sontag writes: "Theories that diseases are caused by mental
states and can be cured by will power are always an index of how
much is not understood about the physical terrain of a disease."

I didn't feel in charge of my metaphors any more than I felt
in charge of my face.

I cupped my hand around the left side of my face to hide, a
new habit, and thought: "Tyger! Tyger! burning bright / In the
forests of the night, / What immortal hand or eye / Could frame
thy fearful symmetry?"

Thud, thud, thud. I couldn't get the meter out of my head.
What did Blake mean by "fearful symmetry"? In the poem, Blake
asks how the creator would make something so fearsome as a
tiger—the last line implying a destructive power in symmetry. I
myself was starting to feel that symmetry contains an element of
dread, because symmetry is powerful and can be taken away.

That August, we went to Rhode Island for "vacation" with our
two babies and four-year-old. The promise of the sea, the sea. We
rented an old farmhouse. It looked like the ceiling might fall in.
The sea, the salty sea. I went in the ocean and braced myself; I
still couldn't completely shut my left eye; and when I swam, the
seawater rushed in. I retreated to the sand, my left eye stinging
with salt, thinking about how underrated blinking is.

Once when I was little I was standing with my father by the
Atlantic. A wave rushed in, and I fell under its power. I struggled
but couldn't get up, and salt water filled my mouth. Suddenly
there was a strong hand pulling me up. The tides were big but
my father was bigger.

Now, not wanting salt water to rush into my unblinking eye, I sat on the sand, sank into the role of the observer, and watched the other swimmers. I jiggled Hope and William, sleeping in their car seats on the sand. I tried not to worry as Anna skirted the edge of the ocean. The sunlight was fierce. When you can't blink, staring into light on a sunny day becomes existential.

I thought about all the hidden perils for the unblinking eye:

A baby putting a finger in your eye.

Putting on a new shirt and realizing that a tag is about to slice into your cornea.

A toddler spraying sand on everyone at the beach.

Kissing with one eye open isn't exactly a peril, but it is strange.

And so I manually shut my frozen eye before kissing my husband.

One comfort is that women's faces almost always look contorted in the act of love. I was no different from any other woman in the throes of ecstasy, I told myself, with my contorted asymmetrical face. Plus, love often happens in the dark.

That summer in Rhode Island, I looked for an acupuncturist for my Bell's palsy. (You know you've had a condition too long when you start using the possessive "my" to describe it.) The acupuncturist I found was also, apparently, a medical doctor in Poland, and he was very authoritative. He told me I should have been going to acupuncture twice a week since the onset of the illness, that once a week would do nothing. He looked at me appraisingly, almost accusingly, saying, "You're still a young woman." He seemed to be chastising me for not taking my disfigured face seriously enough, not doing enough to cure it. He told me to practice whistling at every opportunity. But I could only whistle if I pressed my finger on my cheek to move the muscle, so I played my cheek like a piccolo player. *Whistle while you work,* I whistled. Or: *I whistle a happy tune. . . .*

And I thought, while manually whistling, what did he mean when he said, as though a rebuke, "You are still a young woman." Lots of women feel increasingly undesirable and invisible when they age, I told myself. I'm just an extreme version, a metaphor, if you will, for the mounting invisibility of middle age. There are so many ways to become invisible. One of my actress friends had just turned fifty and started wearing beautiful Hermès scarves to hide the inevitable transformation of neck flesh. I would like to think of the new rings on my neck as rings around a tree, signifying age and wisdom. (A tree acquires one light ring and one dark ring annually, both spring and summer growth. The new rings around my neck were winter growth.) But I also understood the impulse to hide them.

The Polish acupuncturist also told me that my early acupuncture treatments might have harmed my face more than they helped, because the first practitioner I saw did electrostimulation, which in some cases can have a deleterious effect on the nerves. Oops. At any rate, I followed his instructions to the letter. I saw him twice a week while we were in Rhode Island. I tried to whistle. I tried to lift my eyebrows. I tried to blink.

And then . . . that fall, a new milestone: I could blink again. I could blink! No one tells you what a joy blinking is. And then finally one day: Hallelujah!

I still could not whistle, or smile, but *Goddammit, I could blink!* Blink, blink. Blink.

I was full of joy about my blinking. Still, I hated what the effort of smiling did to my face. Extreme effort at happiness is painful to look at in general, and the effort involved in smiling seemed almost to defeat the purpose of the smile freely given. A forced grimace was what registered. My face felt like a system of moving parts: this part moved, that part didn't. I felt like anatomy rather than a whole. And I was beginning to be aware that the extreme effort at smiling created other disturbances. If Bell's palsy does not get better, you may actually start to look *worse* over time, because of the way the muscles try to compensate. When I tried to smile, the muscles in my neck bulged out with effort; my left eye closed almost completely; and the ultimate irony—the left side of my mouth curved down rather than up. Here was an extreme effort of mine to smile with teeth:

And so I did not try to smile widely. To have the face not match the self is a disturbance. But to create a flat inner landscape to match the flattened outer landscape of the face was in retrospect a bad alternative.

I attempted to make myself invisible, like Lucy Snowe. The most flamboyant facial expression I attempted in public was to curve the right side of my mouth slightly up, like the *Mona Lisa*.

CHAPTER 16

Three Children Under the Age of Five and Three Kinds of Vomit

Hope and William, eating.

The strange mathematics of twins. I wanted to spend double the time with them because there were two of them and I thought they deserved two of me. This impossibility tore me in half.

While watching them learn to walk, I felt danger everywhere. I would hold Hope's hand while she practiced walking; and William, on his own, would imitate her, grabbing on to a chair and falling down with the chair on his head. I would rescue William, who was now trapped under a chair; and Hope would find this funny and immediately imitate him, holding on to a chair and falling down with a chair on her head. So I pulled them out from under the chairs, one after the other. The fact that they hit their milestones simultaneously was intoxicating, but also terrifying for a mother who was already anxious about the physical world. Once, strapped into her high chair eating cut-up strawberries, Hope started choking, so I grabbed her, flipped her over, patted her hard on the back, watched her cough the strawberry up onto the floor, then I looked up to make sure William wasn't likewise choking. He wasn't.

Because I couldn't see how to travel with the babies to theater openings and care for them with my mind free to do my rewrites, I stopped doing any theater openings out of town. On the one occasion I'd already committed to an out-of-town production, I told the director I'd come for the first week of rewrites, and the last week of previews, rather than the whole month of rehearsals. And I left all the kids home with Tony and Yangzom. I felt a terrible physical ache leaving; I'd never left them home for longer than two days, and I was still in the process of weaning Hope and William, who were now almost one.

Leaving for the airport—the first time flying anywhere without Hope and William—I felt an awful pang for the first five minutes, then breathed. I relaxed into solitude and my sense of my body as a separate entity. What on earth would I do at the airport with all that free time, with all of those free hands? I might drink *coffee*. And *read*. *At the same time*. It was luxurious.

When I got to rehearsals, I worked steadily on rewrites. I'd written the play before the babies were born, and now came the magical time for realizing language in three dimensions. I welcomed the joy of collaborating with actors again, making up an alternative world in a room together.

Halfway through that first week, Tony called me; William was in the hospital. He'd had a breathing episode. Tony didn't want to worry me, didn't want me to panic and come back early. As a doctor, he felt capable of handling this on his own, but he felt I should know. Premature babies like William have a much higher chance of breathing difficulties and asthma than other babies because they're born with less-developed lungs. Whenever William got a cold, he had trouble breathing, and we had to use a nebulizer on him. In fact, Hope had trouble saying "William" when she first learned to talk, so called her brother "Miyo," which became his family nickname. But she had no trouble saying *nebulizer*—she was so used to seeing its cloudy fog in the living room, hooked up to her brother.

We'd been through croup once with Hope when she was three months old, which was terrifying, but this sounded worse. William was at the hospital in New York, having what they call retractions, grunting while breathing, his whole chest involved in the process. He was diagnosed with respiratory distress syndrome, and was given steroids and albuterol. I was in a state, frantic that William was sick and I was away. Tony encouraged me to stay out of town and finish my work, but I flew home to be with William.

During the week I was gone, the twins had given up on breastfeeding. When I tried nursing them, they just looked me in the eye as though to say huh? and turned away. We were on to bottles. And that was fine. Almost a year of breastfeeding twins had exhausted my body and I had very little milk left to give. When William was all better (the steroids and nebulizer did their job well), I flew back to rehearsals for the last week of previews and opening night. Previews are that magical, anxiety-ridden time when you realize whether or not your play is working in front of an audience. On the night of the first preview, I was incredibly relieved that the audience laughed in the right places.

After the show, we all went to the theater's bar to celebrate. Now that I wasn't breastfeeding, a dirty martini looked awfully good; and the director, a dear friend, clinked glasses with me. In the middle of our toast, the artistic director approached. I thought he might congratulate us—the audience seemed ebullient—instead, he chastised me for being away so much during the rehearsal process. While others drank cocktails and celebrated, the artistic director told me that I was the laziest, most irresponsible writer in the American theater, unwilling to be present and do my rewrites for a premiere. He might not have known at that moment that I'd effectively weaned my twins in order to work at his theater, or that my son had recently been in the hospital. He told me that he was angry with me, that New York might have a good version of my play, but his theater would have a mediocre version, because I hadn't been physically present enough.

I was shocked. Enraged. And I thought: How the hell am I going to do my work in this landscape?

The next morning, the artistic director apologized for his outburst. I like apologies. It's not given in every lifetime to forgive or to be forgiven. And I count every act of forgiveness as a little gem along the stormy path. And so I forgave him. Could my play have been better had I been more present in the room, less torn between motherhood and writing? It's possible. Was it also possible that I ignored some notes I was given, not because I was out of the room but because I didn't agree with them aesthetically? Also possible. At any rate, if I forgave the artistic director (and I did), why cling to his words or write them down at all? I suppose I hold fast to his words in case any leader of a theater, or any leader of another enterprise that employs women, might wonder what it's like to be a breastfeeding mother of twins trying to work out of town.

Back in New York that winter while the twins were still learning to walk, I felt isolated. I wasn't even trying to write. I was just trying to get through the day, and occasionally trying to get out of the house. One day, having been cooped up for weeks, I was determined to get us all outside. It was a cold day and we had all just had the stomach flu.

My three children's temperaments can be summed up in the way that they vomit. Anna vomits dramatically, in full public view. Hope vomits quietly in a self-possessed way; by the time she is three, she will be able to clean up her vomit herself and go back to sleep. William vomits tenderly in bed, over and over again, quietly weeping.

To protect the twins from walking into Anna's vomit, I put them in their high chairs while Anna vomited in sweeping arcs across the kitchen floor. I still have a picture of that event: Anna sitting proudly by her vomit, and Hope just gazing from her high chair at a pile of vomit on the floor. William must be outside the frame: either vomiting or asleep.

But that day, I resolved that we had to get out of the dark apartment. We'd been indoors for a week, and now we were healthy. All that was needed was a destination. We *will* get out of the apartment, I resolved, we must, and go to . . . where? Dunkin'

Donuts. Yes. A modest aspiration. I put Hope's socks on. She took them off. This went on for some time. I put William's snowsuit on. But the snowsuit feet were slippery and he fell and banged his head. By this time, Hope's socks were off again. I screamed, "Goddammit, I can't even get out of the house!"

Anna said, "You're being scary, Mom."

Then I heard a large fart. William had pooped in his diaper inside his snowsuit. I took off his snowsuit. I started to change his diaper in the hallway before leaving. There was no garbage can nearby. I put the dirty diaper on the floor while I changed him. He peed in my face. Then I saw, out of the corner of my eye, Hope crawling towards the dirty diaper. . . .

"No!" I cried. And at that moment I knew: we would not make it to Dunkin' Donuts that day.

CHAPTER 17

All the Crying Mashas and
the Concept of a Good Side

That winter, I found myself watching auditions for my translation of Chekhov's *Three Sisters*. The glorious actors emoted
and I, frozen faced, watched all the crying Mashas. One actress
auditioning for Masha was such a good crier that her tears
seemed to fly out of her face sideways. On the wall behind these
deeply expressive actors was a mirror.

I could see myself watching the actors, and I looked expressionless, a mask. And I wondered: Can one experience joy when
one cannot express joy on one's face? Does the smile itself create
the happiness? Or does happiness create the smile? This was not
only a neurological question, and a Buddhist question, it was also
a question for actors.

Do actors need to experience the sadness in order to express
the sadness? There was once a neurological study done that measured actors' physiological condition after acting. There was no
physiological difference between an actor who had experienced
grief onstage and a regular person who experienced grief. This
made me pity actors.

The Greeks had a mask for comedy and another for tragedy. In
the tragedy mask, the eyes and mouth go down; in the comedy
mask, the eyes and mouth go up. By putting these immutable

masks on their faces, the performers could metaphysically chan-
nel these emotions.

In the 1970s, the English theater guru Ken Campbell developed an approach to acting using the two sides of the faces separately. He wrote, "Like Stanislavsky and Brecht, I've invented
an entirely new method of acting, I call it the enantiodromic
approach. The theory of enantiodromia is that the left and right
sides of your face represent different personalities. If you're
clever with mirrors, you'll see what I mean. My right side, for in-
stance, is that of an inept housewife and the left side—or 'facet'
as we call it—is that of a spanking squire!"

Enantiodromia, according to the ancient Greeks, is a study of
how opposites become each other. The Greek philosopher and
lover of transformation Heraclitus said, "Cold becomes warm,
and warm, cold; wet becomes dry, and dry, wet." Ken Campbell
transformed the notion into an acting style.

I spoke to an actress friend who studied briefly with Campbell
in England and asked her how it was possible to separate the two
sides of her face. She said it was easier than you might think—
that according to Campbell, one side of her face was aggressive
and the other side more passive. If she created awareness of those
natural facial tendencies and exaggerated them, she had, effectively, two characters (one docile, one aggressive) to play with on
her (it must be said, very beautiful) face.

I remember one ridiculous photo shoot for *American Theatre* magazine, back when I could smile, pregnant with Anna. The photographer leaped around, snapping photos and telling me and the other
two women playwrights to smile with our eyes, not our mouths. I
was cranky and hungry. The three women playwrights were grac-
ing the cover that month because our plays happened to be the

most produced that season. The photographer said we should take off our cardigans because it would be better—a warmer look—for women playwrights to "show some skin." Lynn Nottage and I dutifully took our cardigans off. Theresa Rebeck just glowered at him and kept her cardigan on. Good for Theresa, I thought.

The photographer snapped more shots, telling us to cross our arms over our chests, to look tough, and again yelled his injunction, "Don't smile with your mouth! Smile with your eyes!" I thought: I'm not an actress. I have no concept of how to do that.

It's not that I've never acted. I played the warbling, smug sister Mary in *Pride and Prejudice* in seventh grade. At a local community theater, I was Augustus Gloop's sister in *Charlie and the Chocolate Factory*. But, you say, Augustus Gloop never had a sister. Exactly. It was a small part. I studied acting at the famed Piven Theatre Workshop in Evanston, Illinois. I loved being in a state of play with my comrades, but once the audience came, I didn't enjoy performing as much as I should have, had I wished to pursue acting with full-throated confidence.

Playwrights can be strange hybrid creatures. We enjoy our solitary time to write, but we are often champing at the bit to join the fray—to be in a room hearing our words aloud with the more embodied among us: actors. There are at least two kinds of playwrights: those who began as actors who tilt towards the embodied side and do not like as much to be in a writing retreat, and those (I lean this way) who began as poets who have to work up their courage to have a seat at the rehearsal table. But playwrights, like all writers to some extent, are perpetual observers, looking at the moment while they are in it.

* * *

I made a list of all the smiling idioms:

> Wreathed in smiles.
> Smiling from head to toe.
> A ready smile.
> A forced smile, a smile freely given.
> A million-dollar smile. (Like Julia Roberts's smile, which
>   is insured for millions of dollars.)
> Smiling with your whole body.
> Smiling with your eyes.
> Smile and the whole world smiles with you.

> Then I think:

> Her face fell.

Her face fell should mean a thing that happens quickly, then returns to the status quo. But her face, having fallen . . . and fallen and fallen . . . and stayed fallen . . .

When Angelina Jolie had Bell's palsy, it went away almost immediately, returning her to preternatural beauty. She said her Bell's palsy went away because she did acupuncture. I did acupuncture too, without the same results. It could be that she had a milder case. It could be that she did more acupuncture.

Tina Fey, one of my heroes, tosses off questions about the scar she got in childhood, saying that she was a confident child, and would often forget about her scar until she had to be on camera, when she would be shot from her good side.

No one faults Tina Fey for being asked to be shot from the right side because of a traumatic scar, whereas people do fault actors for being asked to be shot on their "good side" because of mere vanity. Rumor has it that talk shows have been asked to flip whole sets so that Barbra Streisand could feature her left profile. Claudette Colbert famously preferred her left side. On-set carpenters frantically rebuilt doorways for her to walk through. Colbert would paint greasepaint on her right side so that cameramen couldn't shoot her unchosen side.

Ariana Grande has been mocked for only being photographed from her left side; one writer even wrote her a letter penned from her right cheek, begging to be seen. Mariah Carey favors the right side. Jean Arthur, too, favored the right side, shunning photographers and publicity, and was often photographed with her right hand over her right cheek.

The concept of a good side implies a bad side. But apparently we are all much more asymmetrical than we think we are. In fact, portrait painters create life and interest in the face by creating asymmetry, rather than exact symmetry.

Rembrandt's self-portraits are divided into light and dark, and the drama of his painting is often developed through asymmetry. I started to think of my face that way: the dark side and the light side. One side going up, the other side going down. When I was a teenager, I loved studying the human face and tried to capture the quicksilver of a soul on paper, fantasizing about becoming a portrait painter. And now I wondered at my own face's opacity— Could a portrait painter now capture my soul by reproducing the current proportions of my face?

When I was photographed during that time, I asked if I might be shot in profile, or on my "good side," which seemed absurdly vain for a writer. My frozen face is on my left side, the side that, theoretically, shows more emotion. Scientific studies have demonstrated that we show more of our emotion on the left side, which is controlled by the right hemisphere of the brain, the half that regulates emotion. Some have theorized that actors often favor their left side as a result.

Does that mean that my affect appeared even flatter than it would if my right side were affected? I always had a bit of a poker face even before the paralysis.

In my early twenties, I dated a man who made films, and I would sometimes humor him by being in a short experimental scene. I remember one time I was supposed to be acting angry, and I did the scene, feeling all kinds of rage. When he showed the film to me later, I appeared to be talking in my usual calm manner, revealing no rage at all. Had I always had a mask over my rage?

My poker face has been helpful in auditions; I don't agitate actors, with their mobile faces and sensitive hearts. Colleagues have occasionally been jealous of my poker face: "How did you acquire that?" they would say. "Years of practice? Temperament? I have no idea what you're thinking." Not revealing what you're thinking can be helpful to a playwright in rehearsals.

Sometimes it is amusing to imagine an actress playing me with Bell's palsy. I imagine her having to Scotch tape her face to make her eye droop and her lip tilt downwards. "How brave you are!" her imaginary makeup artist would tell her. Like Nicole Kidman playing Virginia Woolf, with a bulbous prosthetic nose, which always irritated me. Woolf's nose was never that large, was it? Virginia Woolf was considered beautiful, back in the day. Why must she now seem ugly to write her luminous prose?

People I met who used to have Bell's palsy kept assuring me that mine would be gone any day now. I went backstage to visit an actor friend after a performance and assured her that I loved her performance, even though I could not communicate that with my face. Another actor backstage heard me, and flashed a large white smile in my direction, telling me that my palsy would be gone any day now; he had it once, and it was gone in three

weeks, evidenced by his gorgeous smile. I grimaced with gratitude, grateful at least that I was a writer, not an actor. I didn't tell
him it had been a year.

A beautiful smile is nothing if not a flash, a revelation, of symmetry. The lips are curtains raised on teeth for a brief moment.
Without symmetry, a smile is a smirk, a wince, a grimace. A spontaneous, unthinking, perhaps slightly aggressive flash of teeth—
saying, I will not eat you. But I like you.

We know biologically that symmetry is pleasing; even fruit flies
like it. Apparently symmetrical fruit flies are more sexually desir-
able, to other fruit flies, that is. Studies have shown that college
freshmen and chickens also love symmetry.

Why do we like things to look the same to the left and the
right but not up and down? We don't mind that heads and feet
do not match, but we do not like it if there is a left hand and no
right hand. In movies or plays the one-handed man or disfigured
being is grotesque, an indication of mal-intent. Captain Hook.
Darth Vader. Doctor Poison in *Wonder Woman*. Why are villains
so often asymmetrical? A bloody eye, a mask, a scar, a missing
ear, the Joker. The physical therapist I met told me about a patient with Bell's palsy who looked exactly like the Joker (and
I thought: What cartoon villain do I resemble?). Villains are
not always asymmetrical; they sometimes have altogether blank
faces, like No-Face from *Spirited Away*. Apparently the new cartoon Star Wars villain Darth Nihilus was partially based on No-
Face. These villains with their disfigured, masked, or blank faces
are symbols of opacity, never-ending greed, vengeance, a lack of
stable identity.

But can an asymmetrical person be a protagonist rather than
an antagonist?

In a Jungian dictionary, a one-limbed person is closer to God, concealing a mystery or hidden potential, and signifying the number one, a God number. But where do we put all the asymmetrical people? The asymmetrical stories? Where do we put the people with one leg, lazy eyes, crooked grins? Do we write plays for them? Do we make theaters for them? If symmetry is beauty, but life is asymmetrical, then how can art imitate life with an expression of formal beauty that is also true?

Around that time, I took Anna to karate class and caught sight of my crooked face in the mirror. I thought: *a face only a mother would love.* Then I thought: Oh! Motherhood. Oh the fact of mothers loving all the faces of their children. How beautiful, actually, that concept, couched in a mean phrase. And unbidden, the thought came: Jesus would love my crooked face.

In my childhood, I always thought more about God than Jesus. But now I thought about how embodied Jesus is. We are never allowed to see "the face of God" in this lifetime but we see Jesus's face and hands, we see him walking around in his robes. In Sunday school I would color in pictures of him. He would put his hand on my face gently, I thought.

Then the passage from Paul in 1 Corinthians came to mind: "For now we see through a glass, darkly; but then face to face: now I know in part; but then shall I know even as also I am known."

Even in the afterlife, do we recognize each other by our faces?

CHAPTER 18

Show Me What You've Got

Twins are, in a sense, the ultimate expression of symmetry. Fraternal twins, one male and one female, even more symmetrical. Yin and yang. Doubleness. In literature, they are often used to represent the lost other self—one Shakespearean twin in *Twelfth Night* is lost in a shipwreck, then reunited with her brother. The reunification of that which has been separated results in joy and symmetry. Shakespeare himself had twins, if his biography is true. He had an older girl, and fraternal twins. There are seven mysterious years, called Shakespeare's lost years, in which he did not write. No one speculates that he did not write because he was changing the diapers of twins. Maybe his wife, Anne Hathaway, was, like: you better stop writing those fucking plays and hold a baby for a change. I can't hold two at the same time.

At Hope and William's first birthday, I felt immense gratitude for their health. And rage that my face remained crooked. I should have been much better, or completely healed, a year after diagnosis. I was not better. Most people (85 percent) have Bell's palsy for only three months or so; 95 percent of people are better after a year. I knew that, since I was not better, luck was not on my side for a full recovery. I was in the land of the rare, the unusual, the outlier, the slow boat, the 5 percent, just as I was when I had cholestasis of the liver, which affects only one woman in a thousand.

I remember walking to Gristedes to buy birthday candles, enraged by the marker of time, and by my face, and angry with myself for being angry. I decided that I should probably see that neurologist who I didn't like again.

So I braced myself, got on the subway, and went to the Upper East Side, land of bad news.

Once I was in his office, my neurologist (whose name I cannot remember, as I have an uncanny ability to forget the names of people I don't like) regarded me and said, "Show me what you've got." I looked at him, confused.

"Smile," he said. I tried to smile. Nothing happened on my left side. "Lift your eyebrows." Nothing happened. He looked at me appraisingly for all of thirty seconds. I assumed that he'd at least comment on my limited but incredible progress—I could blink now, after all! A huge achievement! And I didn't drool when I ate anymore. I could even shift food from side to side in my mouth, I told him proudly.

"Are you aware that you have a tic?" he asked.

"No," I said, not pleased that he'd pointed this out.

"You're twitching right now," he said. "I think you should see a neurosurgeon."

"They have surgery for this?" I asked.

"Yes," he answered. "It's in the experimental phase."

"You mean, plastic surgery?" I asked.

"No, this is neurosurgery, baby," he said, rubbing his small hands together.

I couldn't quite believe that he was so excited about neurosurgery that he actually called me baby.

"I'm not sure I want neurosurgery," I said. "I need my brain. To write. And for other stuff too."

He told me I should seriously consider the surgery—that my nerves had reconnected incorrectly, incompletely, and that there is a long Greek word that begins with an *s* to describe what happened to me. I forgot the word as soon as he uttered it, and he told me to see the chief of neurosurgery at NYU.

I explained to him that I hadn't had much rest this year, that maybe I could start to sleep soon, now that I'd weaned the babies, and the rest might help me recover. He said rest wouldn't matter much, not at this point.

He told me that essentially nothing I did would help my chances at recovery: not acupuncture, not physical therapy, not rest. My nerves had grown back wrong, he said, like wires that had gotten crisscrossed. I asked him if surgery could uncross the wires. "Not exactly," he said, "but it's your only option." I did not want to cry in front of this man.

I got up to leave. He told me that he liked my shiny boots. "They're rain boots," I said.

"Well, they're certainly shiny," he said.

I fled his office, full of self-pity. What's more, the rain poured down. I felt justified indulging in the pathetic fallacy—the rain must have been pouring down because it felt self-pity too.

Months passed. I did not call the chief of neurosurgery at NYU.

Instead:

A baby nurse from Barbados, one of the most compassionate women I've ever met, told me to put a whole nutmeg in my mouth on the affected side, and suck on it all day. Which I did.

An Ayurvedic doctor told me to self-massage my face and slather myself in sesame oil. Which I did.

I read in *People* magazine about a celebrity who put a vibrator on her puffy eyes to increase blood flow to the face. I put a vibrator on my face. And decided it worked better for its original purpose.

I got tested for Lyme disease. The results were inconclusive, but I took the heavy-duty antibiotics anyway, now that I'd stopped breastfeeding.

Someone else told me to get B_{12} shots. I got them. They made me feel lively.

I tried Reiki. I liked it. It made me fall asleep.

Someone recommended a chiropractor. He grazed a bristly brush along my cheek and told me to run things with contrasting textures along that side of my face. I did.

Someone else recommended craniosacral massage, and I booked an appointment. The massage therapist said, "I feel nothing, no energy on the entire left side of your body." She seemed frustrated with me, as though I was willing myself to be static.

Yangzom told me she knew of a monk who had been known to cure crooked faces by touch. I said I would be happy to meet him. She searched for him.

Turned out he was dead.

Finally, I decided not to try anything else to help my face. I decided the neurologist with the small hands was right. There was nothing to be done. I simply had to go on with my life, and forget about my face.

CHAPTER 19

The Observer and the Observed

Anne Sterling, Tony, me, and Paula Vogel at my wedding.

I'd never considered a teaching job while the kids were little, but when the twins were a year and a half, I started teaching playwriting at Yale School of Drama. Paula needed to step away from teaching for a semester because of a theater production, and she asked me as a favor to teach. I never said no to Paula. This was the woman who got frocked for the day and with her wife, Anne—who happened to have been Tony's teacher and mentor—married us.

Paula was the woman who cured me of my inability to write after my father died when I was twenty. This was the woman who insisted I get treated for a kidney infection when I was twenty-six and had no health insurance. She gave me five hundred dollars to see a doctor, saying this money had been recirculating for years, given to her by an older woman when she was once a young writer and in need. She told me not to repay her; that when I made five hundred dollars, I should give it to the next young woman writer in need, and so on and so on—the gift kept on giving. And Paula's gifts to me were immeasurable.

So when Paula asked me to substitute teach for her, even though all the kids were small and my physical energy was limited, of course I said yes. And it turned out that teaching held a kind of salvation—a spiriting out of the self towards others that I desperately needed. I would take the Amtrak train to New Haven once a week because it held the promise of the vaunted quiet car, one of the only places on earth where a public official demanded silence. I would wait for the dulcet tones of the conductor: "Please maintain a library-like atmosphere," and I would settle into reading and writing. I would settle into myself.

And it was the only silence I had at that time in my life.

When I met my students for the first time, I was torn between telling them that if I didn't smile at them it's because I had a neurological condition, and pretending everything was normal and letting them assume that I was just vaguely aloof. I decided that the vulnerabilities of my students outweighed my own vulnerabilities, and told them up front about my Bell's palsy, worried that my poker face might falsely indicate dislike, disinterest, or judgment of them, or of their plays. I told them if I looked disapproving while I was listening, it was my face betraying me, not matching my inner life. Sensitive to how raw writers feel when being listened to by their teachers, I added more approving murmurs to my repertoire of listening noises.

I did an exercise with the students so they could get to know each other at the start of the semester. It involves sitting in pairs, having person A look into person B's eyes silently, observing them minutely. Then person B gazes at Person A.

I did this exercise for two reasons—first, it immediately produces the sensation of knowing a person fairly well to gaze into their eyes for two minutes (as proven by that famous love study by Arthur Aron and then deeply oversimplified in popular culture). Second, I wanted students to reflect on how vulnerable they felt when being observed.

I myself find this exercise so uncomfortable—to be in the observed position—that when I do the game, I actually trick myself and pretend I am the observer while I am being observed. This is the only way for me to endure being looked at, particularly with Bell's palsy. The playwright's role of eternal observer has always suited me; I have always preferred looking at others to being looked at. I began to realize that for the past few years, my frozen face allowed me to sink even more deeply into this stance. I had survived social situations by tricking myself into believing that I was merely an observer, hiding in my poker face, holding myself apart, watching. If I tried to mirror my interlocutor's expressive face, I'd make contorted expressions, but if I calmed my face into a neutral observer's face, I could control my facial spasms.

In other words, if I wore a demure and vaguely expressionless mask, many would not guess my deformity. It was only if I attempted a wide grin—letting a viewer more amply into my emotional state—that my asymmetry would be betrayed. Oh—and if I talked. The profound downside of this retreat-to-observer approach was that I probably seemed withdrawn, or aloof. Going a step further—if the body affects the inner life, not only did I *seem* more withdrawn and aloof, but I also *became* more withdrawn and aloof.

And, as a person born in Illinois, I tend to be stung by comments that I'm aloof.

* * *

When I was eighteen and my father had just been diagnosed with cancer, I had terrible insomnia. After months of wandering Providence at five in the morning when all the shops were closed, looking for some signs of life after being up all night, I went to Brown University's psychiatric services, hoping they'd give me some sleeping pills. But I was given an appointment with a therapist who, of course, wanted to talk about how my father had just been diagnosed with cancer, which I didn't want to talk about.

She raised her eyebrows at me and asked me if I talked with my roommate about my father's cancer. "Not really," I said. "We're not very close." The therapist wanted to investigate this further: Why was I not close with my roommate? "We don't have much in common," I told her. "The only album she listens to is the soundtrack of *Stand by Me*. Over and over again."

The therapist pressed on. "How do you think your roommate perceives you?"

I hated this question. "I don't know," I said, shifting uncomfortably and realizing I probably wasn't going to get the sleeping pills I craved.

Then the therapist supplied some possibilities: "Does she think you're aloof? Judgmental? Unfriendly? A snob?"

I went back to my dorm room crying, but with three blue sleeping pills in my pocket and in my head a mantra: *aloof, judgmental, unfriendly, a snob.*

Was it any accident that I grew up wanting to express my rage, and my grief, through the bodies of actors onstage?

During the two hours in the quiet car on the way to and from Yale, I began to write again. I didn't have the attention span to

write in long form, but I thought if I could hold a thought from
the morning until evening, and manage not to fall asleep before
writing it down, I would have a victory over chaos. I wrote those
short essays to keep my mind aloft, without thought of publication, but eventually they became a book called *100 Essays I Don't
Have Time to Write*.

At Yale, I met an extraordinary student named Max Ritvo. He
was twenty when he walked into my classroom, and he seemed
like an ancient sage. He was in remission from a pediatric cancer. He was a brilliant poet, and helped me remember why I ever
wanted to write in the first place. His cancer came back while he
was in my playwriting class. All he wanted to do with the time he
had left was to write. We became close friends and exchanged
long letters that I composed while riding the Amtrak train, to
distract him from chemotherapy. We worked on a book together,
an arrangement of our letters. We shared soup and conversation. After he had a particularly painful lung surgery, we took
a selfie, and it's always struck me how happy we both look. He

looks happy despite being in acute physical pain. I look happy despite the Bell's palsy, partly because half my face was left out of the photograph.

Max taught me more about grace than I ever wanted his young body to know. And he died of cancer when he was twenty-four.

CHAPTER 20

Celiac Disease, or I Remember Bagels

Woman in Blue Reading a Letter

Have you ever seen the painting *Woman in Blue Reading a Letter* by Vermeer? It is one of my favorite paintings, and a reproduction hangs in my bedroom. A pregnant woman stands in profile wearing an indescribably beautiful shade of blue, reading a letter, her head tilted down. I saw this painting in Amsterdam twenty years ago and bought the poster. I lost the poster somewhere on a train, and it is a testament to the Dutch postal service and general human decency that about three months later, the poster arrived, curled neatly in a nice black tube, sent all the way to America by a stranger. So I have always loved my poster for that reason: a lost object was found and returned with human care.

But I've also always loved the painting because a pregnant woman is given a letter: Will she accept? An anti-metaphysical Annunciation. Mary is given a letter: Will she accept? A woman artist is about to give birth—the message is both human and divine—will she accept? She is both full and open; waiting, reading. This painting reminds us that women can in fact read, and that pregnant women also have minds. They are thinking about something, but what?

Most of Vermeer's women have opaque faces, and appear to be calm ciphers. Maybe that's why I like them; they remind me of myself.

All this time I had avoided reading about Bell's palsy online, as though reading about bad outcomes would diminish my hope. But now I started to do research. All that I knew up to this point was that Bell's palsy can be vaguely associated with childbirth and pregnancy, when it is not associated with Lyme disease or a rare genetic disease called Melkersson-Rosenthal syndrome. I now learned that for postpartum women who delivered in the hospital, getting Bell's palsy could also be a function of getting a shingles-like virus at the hospital. It might also have to do with fluid retention, immunity, or blood supply. But the condition remains idiopathic—in other words, a mystery.

Chuck Mee, a brilliant playwright and a friend, wrote about his experience with polio as a child in his memoir, *A Nearly Normal Life*. He vividly describes being in the children's ward, mostly in isolation, seeing, one by one, other children recover and leave. He writes, "With each departure, those who stayed behind felt they had taken one more step backward . . . had retreated that much further from the prospect of recovery. In the field of neurology, there is a nearly tautological saying that the doctors repeat like a mantra: if you are improving, you will improve. The more slowly you improve, the less likely, every day, becomes the prospect of a full recovery."

It had been close to two years now since my Bell's palsy diagnosis. The doctors told me that the more time passed, the more unlikely it was that I'd ever fully recover. I never understood why they insisted on pessimism; perhaps they just wanted me to be realistic.

At this point, I could furrow my brow a little. I thought, of course, my brow furrow came back before my smile. And I could chew much better and say my *p*'s without spitting or sounding like I named my daughter "Ho." But I would still rather smile. I once wrote a play called *Melancholy Play* in which a woman, Tilly, is often melancholy, but in a seductive way. "Cheerful people are the worst sort of people," Tilly says, "they smile and their teeth ring." Now, like Tilly, I found people's smiles slightly insidious, an invitation I could not respond to, even a form of gloating. I started admiring taciturn cultures where it is impolite to smile for pictures or for strangers.

The glossy American culture of open-toothed smiles now felt almost aggressive, like monkeys beating their chests. The world seemed full of horrid gleaming white teeth, gloating symmetries. I went around twitching, my left hand over my mouth.

I was slowly developing a smirk. My dear playwright friend tried to comfort me, saying it's adorable, just like her friend Holly Hunter's half smile. I tried telling myself that my half smile was like Kristen Stewart's asymmetrical smolder in the Twilight series. (Yes, I saw the movies too, after I read the books.) If only I didn't have a droopy eye, I'd definitely be in the movies, making out with a super-hot vampire. Sometimes I comforted myself with the thought that at least I am a writer rather than an actor or a politician, in which case my situation would be not just irritating but entirely disqualifying. Writers are allowed to be craggy and wrinkled, a sign of wisdom. But joyless? Joyless, no fair.

I revisited my superstitions, thinking: so much bounty; three healthy, wonderful children. They got safely out of my body, even though my bile was leaking into my bloodstream. They got safely out of the NICU. There had to be a cost.

I entrenched myself further into my mental Gordian knot, thinking: The Bell's palsy won't go away until I am happy again. But I won't be happy until the Bell's palsy goes away.

Sometimes I thought I felt the nerve growing, like a thread being sewn up my face. A pinprick, a sensation of electricity under my skin. A pulsing. Or like God sketching inside my skin, with an Etch A Sketch or a pencil made out of feathers.

After my first pregnancy, I gained weight like any woman logically would. I thought: I have a new postpartum diet I should market to all women called—Buy Bigger Underwear. Eat whatever you like, and buy bigger pants. Buy bigger shoes. My feet were now a half size bigger; perhaps after giving birth, women simply need to take up more space on this earth. The magazines tell us to shrink back down to our prepregnant bodies, but our bodies want to occupy more ground. Our bodies say: you have given birth. Be large.

But after giving birth to the twins and weaning them, I kept losing weight, though I didn't mean to. The kind of weight where your New York friends say, "You look fabulous," but your Midwestern mom looks at the dark rings under your eyes and your visible collarbone and says, "What's wrong?" This troubled me only slightly. In the world of female vanity, I reasoned: my face is disfigured but my pants are loose.

I got up the courage to see a new neurologist to get a second opinion. This doctor's name I do remember, because he was such a good doctor. Russell Chin was on the young side, had a calm manner, and he took a very thorough history. Instead of saying, "Show me what you got," he asked me to tell him the story in detail of when my face fell down.

Dr. Chin listened to the seemingly most irrelevant details around the edges of my story. I told him the whole story about the lactation consultant. How she said, "Your eye looks droopy," and I had replied, "I'm Irish." He looked up for a moment. "You're Irish?" he asked.

"Yes," I said.

"And you've been losing weight for no reason?" I nodded.

"I'm going to test you for celiac disease," said Dr. Chin.

I never thought joking about my Irish ancestry might present a diagnosis. "What's celiac disease?" I asked.

I had never heard of celiac, or gluten. I came to learn that celiac disease is an immunological disorder in which you can't digest gluten; as a result, your stomach, in effect, attacks itself and wreaks havoc on the whole body, causing things like weight loss and peripheral neuropathy (you can't absorb the vitamins that support the growth of the nerves); extreme fatigue; and can also be associated with an increased risk of cancer. Celiac disease is an autoimmune inheritable condition, and it's possible to have the gene "turned on" by an event like pregnancy. It's also possible to have celiac disease your whole life, undiagnosed.

Dr. Chin ordered me a blood test for celiac disease and electromyography (EMG) for neurological abnormalities. If you don't know what an EMG is, that's good, and I hope you never learn firsthand, because it's a kind of medical torture device. Electrodes are poked directly into your nerves to see how your muscles function. It has to be one of the most painful medical tests ever devised. I went in thinking I would be cool as a cucumber because I'd had so many acupuncture needles in my face. I wasn't afraid of needles. But acupuncture needles are designed *not* to go into the muscle. The poor man who delivered my test ultimately had to suspend it midway through because I was howling in pain.

Then I took the blood test. It was positive for celiac disease.

Dr. Chin gave me the news over the phone and I was relieved to have some kind of explanation for why my nerves might be growing back so slowly. I asked, "So maybe if I don't eat pasta I will be able to smile again?" Dr. Chin said it wasn't quite like that, but that the celiac disease might explain the slow regrowth of my nerves—they were being starved of the B_{12} and other vitamins they needed to grow—what are called trophic factors. I needed an endoscopy to make a final diagnosis.

I had an endoscopy. I had a biopsy. I had celiac disease. I would never eat a normal croissant again.

And here I want to take a pause to remember the old food. The food that cannot be replicated. Because it tastes sad with gluten-free flour. And so, in silence:

I remember croissants.

I remember dumplings.

I remember bagels.

I remember fortune cookies.

I meet actresses all the time who eat gluten-free by choice but are not celiac, and this voluntary diet turns them into superluminous beings with boundless energy and radiant skin. For celiacs, eating gluten free just means you're less likely to die of an autoimmune disease and you have the slightest bit more energy than you used to have—meaning, you don't have to nap every day to function.

Sometimes biology has more compassionate explanations for things than psychology does. When I learned I had celiac disease, I finally had an explanation for my slow to nonexistent nerve growth—I wasn't absorbing my food or vitamins. It was not a psychic wound caused by my anger, my inability to accept my bounty. It was not my fault.

Now I could accept the biological fact that I'd simply had bad luck.

CHAPTER 21

Childhood Illness and the Symmetry of Siblings

I was sick a lot in my childhood; I probably missed a month or two of school every year because of illness. The celiac diagnosis explained that, and also how behind I always was on the growth curve (celiac disease inhibits growth because of vitamin deficiency). I was always dimly aware that other people seemed to have vast stores of physical energy whereas I had very little. And this difference I interpreted as weakness.

Now I knew I was getting very little sustenance from my food; it was essentially passing through me, and my body was in a constant state of hypervigilance or inflammation. As a child, missing weeks of school, on my fifth bottle of pink medicine (usually antibiotics for strep throat), I would prop myself up in my sickbed, tricking myself into a dream state of omniscience. With books, I could be anywhere—back in time (the beloved Betsy-Tacy series by Maud Hart Lovelace) or in some far-flung future on another planet (*A Wrinkle in Time*).

I remember when I was alone in my room, sick, I would often hear a sound out my bedroom window that sounded like this: "Feee—fur . . ." and I assumed it was the seesaw at the playground eight blocks away. I remember vividly sitting in my bed, feeling solitary in a pleasurable way, not lonely, and hearing this sound calling out to me—a sound of childhood pleasures fading—not a call to come play. What a victim of nostalgia I was, even at a tender age. I heard the sound, remembered the metallic grate of the seesaw that went up and down, and wondered how the sound could reach so far, how loud it must have been.

Now, all grown-up, I hear that same sound out my window in another city and another state, "Feee—fur . . ." and I realize that it is a birdcall, most likely a chickadee. I now know that it's not possible to hear the subtle sounds of seesaws that are eight blocks away. Is this a story of revising one's opinion? Or a story of how time may change one's knowledge, but the most vivid childhood feelings remain the same?

How strange it is to grow up. We acquire more knowledge, but such grown-up learning may eddy around the currents of deep feeling that knowledge cannot always change.

Since I was sick more than I was well as a child (sometimes it felt like sick was the normal state of affairs and health was an occasional reprieve), I remember asking my pediatrician with his gray beetle eyebrows about why I got sick so much, why my nose was always stuffed up. "You're lucky," he said.

"Why?" I asked.

"Some people don't have noses." I found this explanation unsatisfactory.

My tendency to get sick separated me from my classmates. Is it a mark of an artist that they are more comfortable as children with adults, and more comfortable as adults with children?

Yes, I was the child with a balled-up Kleenex in a raised hand. The kid who, when another child passed her a poison-pen letter, would correct the grammar and then return it.

* * *

When we were little, my sister, Kate, and I created a strange role-play to parody my sickliness and her enviable stolid athletic health. My sister would call me Beulah and I would call her Burly. Beulah was the name of an ancient second cousin who collected antique valentines and wore a short gray wig. I would call to my sister in a weak voice, "Burly, I can't open this pill bottle, it's too hard for me."

And she would call in a deep voice, "Don't worry, I'll do it, Beulah!" and she would tromp over like a giant and pretend to be so strong that as she opened the pill bottle it shattered, pretending that her steps were so loud she would shake the floorboards.

No one could make me laugh harder than my sister. "Burly," I would whinge in a tepid voice, "I need my antihistamines! I can't open the soup tin! It's too hard! I'm too weak!"

"I'll get them, Beulah!" she would shout, and pretend to be so strong that the soup tin disintegrated in her hands. I would collapse with laughter. At times it felt like much of my childhood was spent in bed while my sister played basketball in the alley. This is an oversimplification. Sometimes I played basketball too, badly.

My sister, Kate, and I sit on a porch in Iowa in the 1970s.

Why is it that two sisters often divide the world between them in this way? Exaggerate their strengths and their defects to make a perfect division between realms? A sort of primal, unspoken noncompete clause? A ridiculous insistence on symmetry. I would be weak, she strong. She would be rational, I emotional. Her hell was uninterrupted solitude; mine was uninterrupted group activities. I was nervous on things like cliffs; she was joyful. Once when my sister and I were hiking together in Ireland, we heard a terrible cry—a young redheaded girl had lost her footing and pitched over a cliff. While I cowered, not wanting to see the dead body, my sister ran towards danger and pulled that girl back from the cliff. The girl ended up only with a broken leg, crying, "Will I miss St. Paddy's day?" My sister ran towards physical danger; I ran away from it. She would save a life; I would write a poem about a life that was taken.

She made up happy songs on the piano; I made up sad songs. My sister would rule the realms of science, the body, laughter, numbers. She would be the consort of extroverts, people who know what to do with balls, how to throw and kick them. I would rule the realm of the arts and books, solitude, make a temple for all of it, and leave my body behind. Did my retreat from the body begin even then, knowing it was my sister's province and I had better retreat? What an absurd "fearful symmetry" I had created; my parents never demanded such a division of spiritual labor— but my sister and I had a silent nonaggression pact. The folly of symmetry. Is this sculpting of sibling realms, this granular differentiation, as important to forming a temperament as Freudian concepts like the Oedipus complex? Do we sometimes marry a proxy version of our siblings rather than our parents?

My sister would become a doctor, a psychiatrist. She would wrestle the numbers down, the science down, so that she could fix other people. She would save lives. What realms did she give

up without her conscious consent? Did she resent our uncon-
scious division of realms?

If only Cain had known he was more of an orchard man, Abel
a fisherman. And here I've spent my whole life thinking I was not
particularly competitive with my sister.

Having three children seemed like a challenge to this bilateral symmetry. I had given birth to a triangle—architecturally, a
very stable structure. But the three children changed alliances
constantly. Sometimes the girls were allies; sometimes the twins
were allies; sometimes all three played together. At times a geo-
desic dome, at other times, a wobbly three-legged table, everyone
screaming.

That fall, we moved from Manhattan to Brooklyn so we'd have
more room for our growing household. Anna was five, starting
kindergarten. I was worried that she would miss our old apartment and her friends in Stuyvesant Town. Before bedtime she
said, "Don't worry, Mama, when we move to Brooklyn all the
movers will just put all our stuff on a platform and drive it all to
Brooklyn. Only I wish we could put our house inside that house.
Or take a piece of our house with us. Maybe cut out one of the
walls in the shape of a heart."

In the new Brooklyn apartment, I sat with a screwdriver, trying
to put together a dollhouse for Anna; I thought it might take the
sting out of moving. I was not good with the screwdriver, and the
prefabricated dollhouse lay in pieces around me.

When I was a baby and my sister was four, my father stayed
up all Christmas Eve putting finishing touches on the dollhouse
he'd made for her. It was white with a green roof. He glued in
wallpaper that matched some of the wallpaper we had in our own
house. I inherited the dollhouse when my sister was done with it.

Kate was not all that interested in playing with dollhouses anyway. She was more apt to be found in the alley, playing with other kids, playing with a ball, big or small, pitching, kicking, or throwing. When I took over the dollhouse, I saved my allowance and collected furniture for it. A teakettle. A dark green faux-velvet couch. A tiny cabinet with latches to hold the dishes inside.

I arranged the tiny people, moved them around, invented stories, made the dolls talk to each other. A dollhouse is wonderful training for a playwright. After our kids were born, I asked my sister if I could have the dollhouse for Anna, who was the right age for it. Kate's stepdaughter was too old for dollhouses at that point, and her young boys weren't interested. Kate thought about it and said, no, it was her house, our father made it for her. But she told me I could have the furniture.

And so the dollhouse with the green roof gathered dust in a basement. Of course my sister and I both wanted the house my father had built. I was a grown woman laying claim to tiny furniture. Dividing realms. She would have the empty house, I would have the tiny furniture with no place to put it. Both useless without the other. The perils and costs of symmetry.

Years later, she cleaned out her basement; found the dollhouse; and, full of self-recrimination, asked if I still wanted it. I no longer did. Perhaps we had both finally grown up.

When Anna entered kindergarten, we moved our furniture from Manhattan to Brooklyn, while my mother-in-law was very sick on the other side of the country. I will never forget the moment when she sent Tony her MRI scans, showing a large tumor in the pancreas. She sent a breezy note with it, like: *probably nothing to worry about, dear, but just wanted you to have a look.* Tony leaned over his computer, looking at the scan, seeing the tumor, and put his hands over his face. As a doctor, he knew at that moment how terrible her prognosis was; knew immediately that she would die in months, not years. And yet, he still had to be her son, not her doctor. His medical knowledge vied with his emotional life, and he wanted to give his mother hope.

We listened to my mother-in-law talking on the phone to her friends, saying in her plucky cheerful Australian drawl, *I'll fight the best that I can, but if I lose, that's it, what can I do, it's on to the next life!* We visited her in California with the children. She had no self-pity, and I only heard her cry once on that visit. A terrible wailing cry. I thought she was in pain and ran to her bedroom. It turned out she'd been on the phone, and learned that one of her beloved dogs had died.

On that visit, she held her granddaughter Hope Elizabeth in her arms, saying, "There is no Elizabeth without Hope."

When we told Anna that her grandmother was very sick, and would die soon, Anna said, "How could God take her? Why can't God fix her, sky to earth? If he's so magical and can do everything, why can he not do that?" I tried metaphysical explanations. Practical explanations. But she kept pressing, *but why, why does she have to die?* I said maybe God wanted to see her. She said, *That's selfish of him.*

Finally, one small comfort: I told her she could get a new dress for the funeral.

Liz died in what she called her liberation bathroom. She had turned one of her kids' bedrooms into a large bathroom for herself when they all grew up and left the house. Now it was the most practical place for a hospice bed. She did not want to die in the hospital. Desperate to get out of the hospital after an experimental surgery that led to sepsis, she got to her house, threw her hands up, said, "Home!" and never said another word. Tony was there with his siblings, holding her as she was dying in her liberation bathroom.

After the funeral, Tony was quiet, not only full of grief but also anger at the loss. I had thought: I may be bad at many things that wives are traditionally supposed to be good at—domestic things—but I am good at grief. I can hold him in his grief. But he did not want to be held. And he did not want to reminisce. If I put up a photograph of his mother in the apartment, he would take it down. He didn't want to look at her.

I asked him once during this time what country he felt he belonged to, given that his parents were both expatriates. He said: *My mother was my country. Now she's dead, and I have no country.*

My mother-in-law, Elizabeth,
in Australia in the 1960s.

That fall was cold and quiet. Anna progressed happily at kindergarten. I tried my best to make friends with other parents, compensating for what I thought was an unfriendly frozen face by murmuring and nodding at parent gatherings.

As the weather got colder, the kids were sick a lot. I found myself constantly going to the pediatrician, a tough, smart woman from a Baltic state, around the corner from us in Brooklyn Heights. I went to her office so often that when she saw me coming, sometimes she would just laugh.

The first time I met her she asked if I had any health issues that she should know about in terms of the children. "I have celiac disease," I told her.

"Is that all?" she asked.

"And Hashimoto's disease," I said.

"Nothing else?"

"Nope," I said.

She paused, looking at me. "But you have Bell's palsy," she said.

"That's true, good eye," I said.

I was demoralized that she'd diagnosed me with nothing more than a quick glance. I could tell that she was pleased she'd spotted it, and her pleasure in her own diagnostic abilities irritated me. I also reflected that my own health mattered at the pediatrician's only because it was relevant to the health of my children.

Of the three sick children that fall, Anna was sick the most. She had constant stomachaches and didn't appear to be growing taller. When everyone else got a virus, and went back to school after two days, she recovered slowly and had high, cycling fevers. One night, Tony and I were out at the theater with Paula and Anne for our anniversary. I was loath to leave Anna home with a fever, but Yangzom was with her, and Tony assured me she'd be fine. I laughed halfheartedly at the play, checking my phone at intermission to see how Anna's fever was. When the curtain came down, I got a text from Yangzom: Anna's fever was a little over 104 and she couldn't seem to swallow. Paula said she'd drive us to the emergency room. Anna was so ill that she could barely wake up to see the doctor. The doctor, concerned, ordered a battery of blood tests. We'd been planning to test her eventually for celiac disease, given its genetic component, but hadn't gotten around to it. But at the ER, they did a blood draw.

Anna tested positive for celiac disease.

You're probably sick of hearing about gluten. We all are. Gluten is used as a punch line on sitcoms now, bringing to mind Brooklyn hipsters, vague questions about rice, and the image of a weird expensive muffin falling apart as you bring it to your mouth. As it turns out, gluten makes food stick together. The bread of life, the sauce of life. When you have celiac disease, the whole world looks like a giant sandwich.

We told Anna she could no longer eat the warm food at the school cafeteria, that we would make her a special lunch every day. Oh, how she cried. We'll put your lunch in a Harry Potter lunch box, I said. She cried. My heart ached for her, and I felt responsible for her shoddy autoimmune genes. Anna's siblings tested negative for celiac disease; they could take freely from the bread basket when we went out to restaurants, and Anna would wail.

Food is a taking-part. Bringing your own cupcake to a birthday party is like bringing your own wine to Communion. Food is one part memory, one part ritual, and one part sustenance. Celiac disease makes you into the ultimate individual in consumer life, so we celiacs are a boon for a niche market in the food industry— our food preferences (which, if not followed, can lead to disease and death) can be monetized.

But what we want is real food, and the feeling of taking part. Food is who makes it, and why.

I remember my grandmother's chicken and dumplings. Thick

broth, the dumplings flavoring the fragrant liquid. I learned to make dumplings with potato starch. I remember matzo ball soup, the only food I could eat after my father died. I learned to make it with quinoa flakes. Food is memory, and food is also present-day Communion.

Speaking of ritual, what, asks the Catholic, is to be done about Communion for celiacs? What if Anna ever wanted to take the Sacrament? Some radical nuns in Ohio have apparently made a host out of rice crackers, but according to the Vatican, every Communion wafer has to have a certain amount of wheat in it to make it authentic. Celiacs have to make up their own food rituals.

I think of Proust and the madeleines that unlocked his memory. Is it enough to remember beautiful food with beautiful words? For me, a grown-up writer, memory and words can satisfy. But for my daughter it was different. She'd never had a madeleine.

So, I decided to make madeleines for Anna that she could eat. I bought a tin, found a recipe. Fresh grated lemon peel, almond flour, buttermilk, butter. They puffed up beautifully in the oven and filled the kitchen with the smell of lemon and vanilla.

I put them in her lunch box. And I closed the lid.

CHAPTER 22

Can You Have Postpartum Depression Two Years After Having Babies?

I knew that I loved my husband when we were housemates in graduate school. I knew that I liked living with him. I knew it felt like home. The old pink Victorian house we shared with another student was drafty and cold, and before my then room-mate/now husband left for medical school in the morning, he would check on the temperature of my room. If it was too cold, he turned the space heater on and crept out. How sexy I found his caretaking! Sometimes I would wake up and the heater would be on and a cup of coffee would be outside my bedroom door. How sexy! How cozy! Is there a word for sexy-cozy? Some kind of word in Dutch maybe? Don't look at that man riding a motorcycle. Look at that man shoveling the snow who just gave you the gift of a snow scraper for your car, which was the very first present my now husband gave me when he was only my roommate. Sexy-cozy! The opposite of dirty-sexy!

I knew that I was very happy in this house, this pink house in Providence in which I felt, for the first time in a long time since I had lived in my childhood house, that I was home. I noted that the house seemed less happy when Tony was gone. Before our romance began, when we were merely housemates, his gifts for me evinced practical caretaking; that cold winter, I wore my grandmother's vintage coat until its lining was in rags, and Tony had the coat relined.

I told my teacher Paula that I was fond of my new housemate. Separately, Tony told his former biology teacher Anne that he was fond of his housemate. Somehow, Paula and Anne put together that we were each other's housemates and roared with laughter. Two students who they knew separately, who had each come of age under their care, were cohabitating.

I knew I loved my husband when he came to see an early play of mine. I remember looking around at the audience, but being curious only about what was inside Tony's head. He had loaned me for the evening a Thai Buddhist talisman from his father—a necklace that he said I could wear to opening night as a good luck charm. I found it moving that he would so casually loan me a family heirloom. And as I watched the play that night, I clutched the heirloom for good luck, and watched Tony's face, trying to read it. I loved the quickness of his mind, how keen his perceptions were, how he synthesized the realms of science and art, made a bridge between the body and the mind. We would go to dinner, discuss the blood-brain barrier, the opacity of minds. We would pick Concord grapes in the backyard and make jam. He could cook! He made me delicious soups. And I left poems around the house for him.

One night, he was reading the *New England Journal of Medicine* in bed and I came home from a night drinking Irish whiskey with fellow playwrights in graduate school. "Play with me!" I said.

"I'm reading," he said.

"Dance with me!" I said.

"It's late," he said. I jumped on his bed. He looked up from the *New England Journal.*

That was that.

And how gently he touches my face.

* * *

At our wedding, me wearing my grandmother's old coat.

When the twins turned two, I made two different cakes, as usual, and invited some neighbor friends over to celebrate. With chronic illness, symbolic occasions can be an irritating marker of time passing. Time passes unnoticed, until there is some holiday or anniversary, like the twins' second birthday. I thought: surely I'd be better by now, it's been two years.

I reasoned that now that I knew celiac disease was impeding my progress, and now that I was eating fake toast that tasted like nothingness, I should be absorbing my food and all my vitamins and so my nerves should grow back. But I still wasn't improving. I'd hit a plateau. Time is tricky; time is slow. The nerve grows a millimeter a day. It had now been about 730 days.

When the twins were toddlers, Tony saw that I was overwhelmed by domestic life, and started making grocery lists for the week. He started doing all the shopping, all the cooking. He made playdates for Anna. He braided the girls' hair. He was better at braiding than I was, it turned out. When we walked in Brooklyn, a passerby would admire Anna's braids, giving me an approving

comment, and I would say, "My husband did the braid," elicit-
ing an *ooooh!* Tony's always enjoyed a logistical challenge and a
smoothly running household. He was patient with me.

At the time, I felt full of rage and helplessness, but told no
one. Not even my dear friends, my mother, or my sister. For them
I tried to preserve the illusion of a plucky no-nonsense attitude.
And my rage wouldn't show on my face even if I wanted it to.
After all, I didn't believe in the benefits of rage.

In my twenties, I took a Buddhist meditation class about anger.
We were told by our teacher that it wasn't good to be angry. I
kept pressing: But what about political anger? Shouldn't we have
that? Isn't political rage helpful, in fact necessary to the cause of
social justice? (This was during the war in Iraq, and I was angry
about the war and doing a good deal of protesting.) My teacher
would tell me that the anger was not necessary, that I could take
political action without being angry, and in fact anger does not
fuel right action. He told me that the antidote to the poison of
anger in classical Buddhism is patience. But what about the political value of impatience? What about Audre Lorde's reclamation,
symphony, and call to action in her brilliant essay "The Uses of
Anger," in which she says, "Anger is loaded with information and
energy." I pushed my meditation teacher—asking why he thought
anger could not be fuel for political urgency.

My teacher calmly told me that in Buddhism it is said that one
moment of anger has the power to extinguish years of positive
karma. Certainly, if one murders in a rage, years of doing good
are extinguished in one moment of violence. Once, in Tibet,
he said, a monk was released after years of torture in a Chinese
prison. The monk said he was relieved to be released because he
was on the verge of doing something really awful: he was on the
verge of thinking of his captors without compassion. This, for

the monk, would be the ultimate loss, worse than losing his own life—it would be spiritual devastation.

I noticed at some point that the word *anger* is literally contained in the word *stranger*. How can we use our anger for the cause of justice, or to direct the course of our lives, so that it does not make us strangers to ourselves and to others? Certainly I've had moments of rage where I've felt a stranger to myself, unrecognizable.

And the anger I had at that time in my life was not particularly visible, even to myself, and yet it made me unrecognizable.

Around this time, my father-in-law married a much younger Thai woman whose cranial nerve had been severed ever since she'd been an infant (she'd had a rare cyst that necessitated surgery). My father-in-law (not always the most sensitive) told my husband, "be nice to your wife; Bell's palsy can seriously affect a woman's self-esteem."

And indeed, my new mother-in-law, about my age, told me that Tony's father had changed her life with his acceptance of her face. At a family party, I overheard someone say offhandedly that my father-in-law's new wife was lucky to marry Charlie even though he was much older; that in Thailand, no man would have married a woman who was disfigured.

Disfigured, I thought. Am I disfigured? Then I thought: Couldn't we change the word *disfigured* to something else? Like simply: *asymmetrical*, which is objectively descriptive and devoid of moral or aesthetic judgment.

To disfigure, from the fourteenth century: to mar the figure of, impair the beauty, symmetry, or excellence of.

There is a slippage, even in the dictionary definition, from beauty to excellence. The very definition of the word *disfigure* moves from the beautiful to the imagined moral groundwork for the beautiful. Symmetry feels not only beautiful but *moral* to us. An expression of the balance and harmony of the soul. According to nineteenth-century physiognomy, the structure of the face could tell us about a subject's moral imperfections. I wondered what moral imperfections were revealed by my palsy.

I hadn't spontaneously grinned, showing teeth, in more than two years. I actually didn't remember what it felt like. I felt ugly when I tried to smile with teeth, so I had stopped trying. It was, ironically, only when I openly expressed joy that I looked "disfigured." I hadn't dreamed of smiling in a while either. I didn't try to make expressions that would convey reactions or understanding when people were talking; instead, I nodded.

In essence, I had given up.

In early spring, Yangzom went to India with her mother for two months on a religious pilgrimage to see all the holy Buddhist sites. And at home in Brooklyn, I began to unravel. I cried for no reason. But at the time, I was able to concoct plenty of reasons.

I thought: sleep deprivation was the reason I felt so numb. Or being diagnosed with two new autoimmune disorders and not being able to eat dumplings was the reason. Or having Bell's palsy and not being able to smile was the reason. Or not writing enough was the reason. I didn't have postpartum depression with Anna. I thought I was constitutionally incapable of having postpartum depression—after all, I'm from the Midwest and I love children. I thought: when the children all sleep through the night, I'll be fine. Or when they all go to kindergarten, I'll be fine.

When Yangzom left, I feared being alone with all of the children, feared the moment when the twins cried at the same time and I couldn't comfort them both. I felt deeply inadequate.

At bedtime, sometimes with three kids wailing, while Tony was working late, I would literally crawl into one crib and then crawl into another to calm the twins down while they yelled for a bottle, "Milk baba, milk baba, water baba, water baba!" Then Anna would scream from her room that she was scared to go to sleep by herself and needed me. I would dash from one room to the other.

When Hope and William graduated from their cribs to toddler beds, I would lie down with them at night; and one after the other, they would run out, delighted. As soon as I put one twin back to bed, the other would run out of the room with great excitement. Sometimes they would run into the room I ostensibly used for my office and lock it from the inside, screaming with laughter, "Locka the door!"

During the day, the twins would often push each other off my lap, saying, "Only Hopie," or "Only William." They each wanted time alone with me. Then Anna would get on board my lap, push them both off, and say, "Only Anna." This game was funny but also serious. I wanted to clone myself for each of them, offer each of them a version of me that was not stretched, that was made abundantly and just for each of them. I was trying to make of myself a raft for each child, and I often felt like dead wood.

Looking back, it was my stratospheric expectations that I be a perfect mother, schooled in the excesses of attachment parenting, that helped seal my sense of failure. If only they had handed out a book by Donald Winnicott at the NICU that laid out his incredibly helpful concept of "a good enough mother." Instead, I was inundated by external examples of unachievable perfect parenting and my own internal image of the mother I had been when I had only one child. In retrospect, the mother I was with only one child probably gave *too* much attention; I was the hovering, anxious, clucking mother hen, running after Anna on the playground. And yet I longed to give my three children that single-minded attention. This was existentially impossible, but still, I strove for it. I also measured myself against imaginary mothers who had unlimited supplies of physical energy, boundless optimism, and knew how to sew buttons onto clothes.

Tony was worried that I wasn't leaving the house, that I wasn't writing, and that not writing was making me feel crazy. He told me to go away for a long weekend to write, to finish a play I'd been slowly working on, *Dear Elizabeth*, an adaptation of the letters between Robert Lowell and Elizabeth Bishop—the same letters that I'd been so taken with when on bed rest. The constant interruptions were dogging my ability to finish the play. Tony suggested my mother could come and help out for a long weekend while I wrote.

My mother came. I kissed everyone goodbye, physically full of dread at the thought of leaving the children, and drove to a bed-and-breakfast in Massachusetts. For two strange days, I experienced solitude again, and wrote madly. Then I got a call from Tony: everyone in the house had caught the same stomach bug; everyone was throwing up; he was drowning in it, and he could use my help. So I finished my play in two days rather than four and came home to hugs and a great deal of vomit.

It was not that there was not much sweetness with the children during this time. There was an abundance of sweetness. But I often felt I was observing it from a distance, rather than participating in the sweetness. I told myself that writers are always looking at things from a distance.

And I was so exhausted I felt like a dirty sponge that had been wrung out to dry.

At some point, secretly, I began to fantasize about the new energetic, symmetrical, highly domestic wife my husband would have after I erased myself. This would be a noble self-sacrificing act, I thought. That way my husband would have an equal partner, and not a dragging lachrymose one. I imagined someone like Maria from *The Sound of Music*. She would be a little younger than me; she would appreciate the arts but not be consumed by them; she would take the kids out of doors to fresh mountain air; she would make playclothes out of curtains and be lovely and nurturing; and her smile would be beatific.

I worried that Anna would notice my absence and be scarred by it, but the twins, I reasoned, were too little and likely wouldn't remember me. In retrospect it seems *insane*, but at the time it all seemed highly rational.

I didn't think of these fantasies at the time as postpartum depression. No one even screened me for postpartum depression after I had the twins. One doctor screened me for stress, but not for depression. In other countries, they think of the fourth trimester as applying to both mothers and babies, so they check on mothers shortly after giving birth and automatically screen for depression. I had been so busy paying attention to the twins' basic survival after giving birth that I gave very little thought to myself. But in retrospect I had all the symptoms. The *post* in postpartum depression stood for postponing my own joy; it also stood for crying jags, rage, moodiness, and the feeling that I was unable to care for my babies.

Could you even have postpartum depression two years after giving birth? Or could you slowly develop it until it reached an apex two years later? Could that still count as postpartum depression or was it just depression-depression? How can you ignore postpartum depression for that long, writing it off as lack of sleep, or as a prolonged adjustment to other medical difficulties?

In the medical literature, the baby blues is differentiated from postpartum depression by duration. The *baby blues*, a phrase I cannot stand, is supposed to last only a month or so, whereas postpartum depression encompasses the following symptoms:

Persistent, sad, anxious, or empty mood (check)

Irritability (check)

Feelings of guilt, worthlessness, hopelessness (check)

Lack of interest in pleasure from hobbies (I had no
hobbies, check)

Fatigue (check, check, check)

Difficulty concentrating (check)

Difficulty sleeping (nope, I slept too much)

Persistent doubts about ability to care for the baby or
babies (check)

Thoughts about death (check)

I didn't tell anyone about these thoughts. I was ashamed of them. I had three healthy, beautiful children who were now two, two, and six. And I had a husband who was more than an equal partner. To complain would be sour grapes, the height of self-pity. I was so lucky, I kept telling myself.

When I look back at my journals from this time, what stands out is my love for the children and the joy I took in all the things they said and did. I wrote down things like: *Today William said, "I love you more than a million whales."* How to reconcile that mother, who delighted in everything her children said and did, with this other private mother, who was full of self-loathing, who wanted, on some level, to erase herself? Two sides of a face—one happy, one incapable of expression? A Jekyll and Hyde effect?

One day I was clearing up dinner. I'd cooked something un-remarkable. (I'm not the best cook.) Tony got home late, and my friend Kathleen was over. She peppered Tony with questions about his day at work. She was listening to him empathetically, *the way I probably should,* I thought. I cleaned up while they talked. I realized that it had been some time since I'd listened well, made him feel seen at the end of a long day in which he, a child psychi-atrist, had listened to others, sometimes for ten hours straight.

But in my rattled state, I did not feel self-reproach for my inability to listen—but instead a rage, out of nowhere.

I banged around, cleaning, while they talked, thinking, no one asked me how my day was. *How was your day?* I asked myself, banging dishes into the dishwasher. I'd had some theater disappointment that day—a production canceled. *How was your day?* I thought, bang, bang, bang. But primary in my mind was not the theater disappointment: it was that I felt invisible; I hadn't gotten the pro forma: How was your day with the kids? I felt like the role of housewife had displaced my identity as a writer, and a raw, hot despair built up in my chest. I turned the dishwasher dial to *normal* (feeling anything but), announced abruptly that I was going on a walk, and left the apartment. Tony later said that it looked like a complete physical non sequitur—that one minute I was there, then I wasn't.

I walked briskly down towards the water in Brooklyn. Water is where I always go when I need solace. I walked down High Street sobbing my eyes out, in a kind of delirium, not caring who saw. I walked towards Brooklyn Bridge Park, which curves along the East River. It was twilight, and I could see that on the shore, some park official was renting out kayaks, one of many new absurd gentrifying enterprises in Brooklyn.

I thought: I'll rent a kayak, and I'll just row or paddle until I'm out in the ocean and no one can find me in the dark. It wasn't exactly stones-in-my-pocket Virginia Woolf thinking—it was more mysterious—like an Agatha Christie vanishing act—I'd wash up on some other unseen shore . . . Staten Island? I approached the kayak line, only to realize that I hadn't brought my wallet with me, and, what's more, rentals were stopping for the night. So I sat on a bench and bawled my eyes out.

Tony called me, worried, asking where I was. I told him I was near the water because I thought it might be a nice night to take a kayak ride. "A kayak ride? Where exactly are you?" he asked.

I described the bench. "Stay where you are," he said. "I'm coming to meet you." I needed to be met, and he knew it from the sound of my voice. Kathleen stayed with the children while Tony found me on my bench. He put his arm around my shoulders and walked me home.

In *Melancholy Play*, a character proclaims:

"When someone in your social circle becomes so melancholy that they stop moving, it is your duty as a human being to *go find them*. It is not enough to seek medical attention. It is not enough to ask them how they are feeling. You must go where they are and *get* them. It is up to *all of us* to save Frances. It is part of the social contract."

In the play, melancholy is distinguished from depression; melancholy is a state that can still be aesthetically enjoyed—looking at the rain out the window, say. If melancholy is romantically looking out an open window, depression is lying next to an opaque window locked shut. No one can see you inside. One character in the play, Frances, begins as melancholy but ends up so depressed that she turns into an almond. Yes, a nut. (It's a comedy.)

All my life, I had been no stranger to melancholy, but I'd never been properly depressed before, inert in that way, a stranger to my own thoughts in that way. But by that early spring, I was on the verge of becoming an almond. Still, expressionless, inert, hermetic, and dried out. As Susan Sontag writes in *Illness as Metaphor*, "Depression is melancholy minus its charms." Depression is also woefully hard to write about. It plays with one's memory. Remembering scenes of depression is something like remembering the condition of sleeping without dreaming. There is very little to say about it.

Have I mentioned that my husband is a psychiatrist? He convinced me to go see one.

* * *

Saint Augustine's *Confessions*, arguably the first memoir in the Western world, was a confession of sin. He went whoring, confessed to us about it, and in doing so, gave birth to a new self, along with a new genre. *Confessions* presumed that sin was necessary to the transformation, to grace, and I've always disagreed. I've always preferred Montaigne's discursive reflections to Augustine's self-revelations. But here I am telling you that I went to a psychiatrist, where I must have (one assumes) made some confessions.

Must I have sinned to have earned my right to confession?

Do you think I am avoiding talking about my psychiatrist? Of course I am. But he is an extraordinary man. He listens without judgment, he focuses on health rather than neurosis, and he assures me that I am going to get better. He is also a writer, which I like. And a Buddhist, which I also like. And, under his care, I slowly get better.

As a self-sufficient Midwesterner, I would like to say that I got better on my own. That I philosophized my way out of my dark cave. Or gardened my way out. Or wrote my way out. But I don't garden. And I don't think philosophy, or even writing, can pull people out of those particular kinds of wells. Other people can. And some medicines can, some of the time. Was it the small dose of medicine I took that made me better, or was it the medicine of allowing myself to be seen, to be listened to? Or some complex combination of both?

Was it possible that before treatment, I didn't have enough serotonin in my gut or in my brain? That because I had celiac disease, which prevents the absorption of essential vitamins, my brain was not adequately absorbing that wonderful happy molecule?

Some Swedish researchers found that people with celiac disease have an 80 percent higher risk of depression. Was it possible that my depression was not "my fault"? And why would I have thought it was my fault to begin with? Was I not that different from my mother, who thought any illness was somehow her fault?

I have a clear memory of when I first felt bodily pleasure again during that time. I was sitting by a window in my kitchen. It was the beginning of spring, and a warm breeze blew in. I felt the breeze on my shoulder, and I experienced the warmth as pleasure. I noted how long it had been since I had felt a sensation of pleasure—the kind of pleasure that slows down time, that plants the mind back in the body like a bulb in the earth.

CHAPTER 23

Refuge

Three years after my diagnosis of Bell's palsy, I thought: I am done trying to make my face better. I am done with my body. I am bored with recovery. I have a mind. I am going to go on living my life. And I did. I taught. I wrote plays. I put them on. I turned an old play into a new musical. I published one book. Then another book. I signed books. I took my children to the playground. Tony returned to practicing aikido, a martial art he had always loved but lacked time for when the kids were tiny. We started to sleep in on the weekends while the kids woke up early and watched television. We had parties at our apartment, sometimes with young musicians Tony found who played jazz sets. We dressed up for Halloween—all five of us as Star Wars characters, me as Yoda.

I became persistently, constantly, busy. What I perhaps did not realize at the time was that I decided to move ahead with my life without my body, without my face. I was a disembodied whirlwind. I did not pray for resignation or acceptance, I merely kept moving.

Ever since I was eighteen, and my father was diagnosed with cancer, I felt I could not pray for an outcome. When my father received his diagnosis, and already had stage four cancer, I was pretty sure he would die in the near future. He could barely walk. To pray for his miraculous recovery when I was an agnostic felt impossible. But even as a Catholic, it felt ignoble, blasphemous. I should pray, I thought, for the courage to accept his sickness. I should pray for his peace of mind, but not for an outcome. In the back of my mind, I knew, if I prayed for an outcome, a miraculous return of health that did not come, it might tip the balance of my faith, which was already not sturdy. It would turn me from an agnostic to an atheist. No, God does not intervene in bodily affairs, I thought as a teenager.

I refused to think of prayer as gambling. As in: Please, God, let me roll a three and not a six. As someone raised Catholic, I thought it was possible to get in trouble just for praying wrong. Flannery O'Connor wrote in her prayer journal:

> My dear God . . . It takes no supernatural grace to ask for what one wants and I have asked . . . but I don't want to overemphasize this angle of my prayers. Help me to ask You, oh Lord, for what is good for me to have, for what I can have and do Your service by having. I have been reading Mr. Kafka and I feel his problem of getting grace.

The hope to obtain grace—something that cannot be *gotten*, but received, unbidden—can it even be asked for?

I recently met the theologian Serene Jones. She wrote in her book *Call It Grace* that her father once said, "God comes to us, even though we can't reach God. . . . That's love." As I talked to Serene over dinner, I noticed something familiar about her face. Sure enough, she told me that she'd also had Bell's palsy. Hers had resolved almost completely.

We talked about our experiences, and she told me that one of the things she hated most about not being able to smile was tending to a multiracial congregation, and suddenly being transformed into a white woman who was not smiling but instead grimacing. The smile, she said, has the potential to be disarming, particularly between people of different races, cultures, and faiths.

Jones writes that according to Calvin, the French theologian, the purpose of prayer is not a thing to be gotten, healed, or fixed, but instead "a simple but constant practice of consciously lifting up our messy, mixed-up, hard-hearted lives before God, and in doing so, knowing that God is present."

As a grown-up—I could not pray to God for my face to get better. Not only did it seem faithless, it seemed vain, considering all the trouble of the world.

Is that too some kind of strange internal renunciation?

Simone Weil, a mystic, philosopher, and fighter for the French Resistance during World War II, wrote about grace over and above effort and the will. I have always loved her notion of attention instead of a strained effort to receive grace. Some of Weil's more extreme prayers verge on what I might call a deeply Catholic masochism, particularly the one where she prays, "Father, in the name of Christ grant me this: That I may be unable to will any bodily movement . . . like a total paralytic. . . . May this body move or be still with perfect suppleness or rigidity in continuous conformity to thy will."

This prayer is inexplicable to many, and to me now, after experiencing paralysis—almost unimaginable—that anyone would pray for paralysis as submission to God's will. Catholic masochism has never held much appeal for me, and I have always been less interested in sin than in compassion. In reciting the Lord's Prayer as a child, I was taught to accept the will of God, to intone, "Thy will be done. . . ."

Recently, I was shocked to realize how little I'd impressed

upon my children the power of the Lord's Prayer, which comes to me second nature at moments like turbulence on planes.

I asked Hope where she thought the phrase "Give us this day our daily bread" comes from and she paused, thought hard, and said, "Pain Quotidien?"

(For those of you who haven't eaten there, Le Pain Quotidien is a Belgian chain restaurant that specializes in pastries and fresh bread.)

This is my same daughter who said, when she was making out her Christmas list: "I've decided it's more worthwhile to pray to Santa than to God, because Santa gives you stuff and God doesn't."

Do I blame America? Or myself?

Making lists can be a form of prayer, but I do not make lists of things I want. One day I made a list of things I dread:

Having to look at myself in a mirror while getting a
    haircut, particularly if the hairdresser talks to me and I
    have to reply and see my mouth moving in the mirror.
Sitting at a restaurant with a mirror facing me and having
    to watch myself eat.
Being asked to take a selfie with a stranger.

I also made a list of advantages of having a disfigured smile and I could only think of one:

No one ever sees if you have food stuck in your teeth.

I also made a list of my milestones:

I can drink out of a cup with a thick rim and not drool.

I can eat a piece of toast with peanut butter on it and not
  have food smeared all over my face.

I can take a large bite of apple.

I can laugh in public and almost not feel like a pirate.

I still can't whistle. But I can slurp up gluten-free
  spaghetti.

Meanwhile, my children hit their milestones:

William and Hope learned to swim.

They both lost a baby tooth on the very same night.

William wrote his first sentence: "Hopie is a rat."

Tony taught Anna to ride a bicycle.

Hope learned to do a cartwheel.

My mother taught Anna to knit.

Anna got her yellow belt in karate, a significant
  accomplishment for a child with celiac disease who
  had only recently realized that she'd never run at
  full strength because she'd never had the physical
  energy.

And Tony hit new milestones. At aikido, he lofted other
  bodies into the air, wearing white, rolling, sparring—
  combining strength and gentleness—and he tested
  into a new level, third kyu.

We celebrated our tenth anniversary. Tony invited a magician
friend I'd met through the theater to come to our apartment.
The magician made my wedding ring disappear in a ring of fire,
and then reappear on the Brooklyn Heights Promenade, dan-
gling from a metal globe.

  And in this way, time passed.

* * *

In the midst of all of this living—parenting, writing, teaching, marriage-ing, rehearsing—and basically ignoring my body because it was a source of disappointment, I started getting tingling in my hands and feet that would come and go. Sometimes a strange sense of imbalance, clumsiness. A mysterious passing tremor in my hands.

One day I found myself running for the train after teaching at Yale. I was determined to be home on time for dinner that night; I had promised the children. They had never liked my long teaching days; and Anna, now in third grade, had been going through a bad bout of separation anxiety, exacerbated by my being gone at night to watch previews of a new play. She would cry at school drop-off, not letting go of my hand, screaming.

So when I looked up at the departures and arrivals sign that day in New Haven and saw that my train was about to pull out from the station, I ran like a madwoman down the long corridor, wearing a heavy backpack full of books. I ran at the limit of my physical powers of endurance. I reached the platform stairs, ran up with ten seconds to spare, when suddenly—my legs gave out.

It's not that I tripped. It was an odder sensation. My legs simply gave way, buckled, and I found myself prone, smack down on the stairs, pinned by my backpack like a cockroach.

An older woman helped me up, and I managed to get on the train, thinking: What the hell is wrong with my body?

Worried that there was something profoundly the matter with me, I saw my neurologist, who did all kinds of tests, and cautiously pronounced me, for the moment anyway, fine, with a benign essential tremor. Tony said that I simply might not have had the muscular strength to run up a flight of stairs at full throttle carrying twenty pounds of books on my back. (Beulah!!!) Certainly I'd not been exercising since the twins were born. But a feeling dogged me of something not being quite right. (From *Madeline*: "Miss Clavel turned on the light and said, 'Something is not right!'")

So I did what I tend to do when Western medicine doesn't have answers for me, and I looked for a good acupuncturist, this time in my neighborhood of Brooklyn. I decided it was no longer worth it to take needless trips to Manhattan for anything but highlights or mammograms.

The new acupuncturist's name was Zoe and she was hilarious, and also a writer. So we could talk shop while she put needles in me. At that point I'd given up thinking that my face could ever get better, so I talked to her instead about falling down, the pins and needles, my body somehow saying—enough is enough, I need attention, you've been ignoring me for years now.

Zoe listened with the mind of a detective writer—putting the pieces together—and encouraged me to try to work on the Bell's palsy as well as my other complaints with acupuncture. Though most medical practitioners had told me my face was done getting better after all these years, Zoe was not convinced. She gently put needles into my face once a week. And every time I lay down on her table before getting needled, I felt sensation on the left side of my face.

Were my nerves giving me a Pavlovian response to the promise of stimulation? I could never tell whether sensation on that side was a good thing or a bad thing, evidence of nerve growth or of a spastic twitch. But I chose to believe it was growth.

After two months of seeing Zoe, one of my teeth on the left side was revealed when I smiled.

A tooth, a tooth!

How slowly does the body grow?

The new tooth revealed gave me a certain amount of euphoria.

It used to be that if I wanted to approximate a smile with teeth, I had to use both hands: one to pull the left bottom lip, the other to pull the upper lip, and another finger to pull the corner of my lips to the side. Now I could approximate an openmouthed smile in the mirror with only one finger dragging my cheek up.

As the ability to express joy grew, so too grew my capacity for feeling deep, embodied joy. Something about that second front tooth made the partial smile appear to stand in for the intention of happiness, if not happiness itself.

Sometimes you write a play and it teaches you a way back into your life. That year, I wrote a play called *The Oldest Boy* based on a story Yangzom told me. We were chatting in the kitchen, and Yangzom told me a story of her friends in Boston who owned a restaurant and had a two-year-old son. One day, Tibetan monks from India appeared at the restaurant. After consulting oracles and dreams, the monks had determined that their boy appeared to be a reincarnation of a high Tibetan lama (or teacher) and would therefore need to be educated at a monastery in India in order to reach his full spiritual potential.

"My God, what did they do?" I asked Yangzom.

"They gave the child to the monastery," she said matter-of-factly. She said that they were honored, that it was hard, but of course they must give the child to the monastery or the child would have bad luck all his life. In this lineage of Tibetan Buddhism, a monk will actively search for the reincarnation of his former teacher who died. I decided to write a play about this phenomenon.

As research for the play, I read an entire suitcase full of books about Tibetan Buddhism and about reincarnation. I interviewed lamas. I interviewed monks. I interviewed Yangzom. She became my teacher.

Slowly, what I had thought of as research changed me. What

seemed like a fairy tale when I first heard about it now seemed quite different. I started meditating more.

Is the self the face? A person, their personhood, comes to be associated with their face, a signifier for identity. A person is not their arms or their legs; a person is their face. But what if we are not even our faces?

Shantideva, the eighth-century Buddhist monk, once wrote: "The teeth, the hair, the nails are not the 'I.' . . . If such a thing as 'I' exists indeed, then terrors, granted, will torment it. But since no self exists at all, what is there left for fears to terrify?"

I started to wonder if my fixation on my broken face could be helped by a focused attention on the illusion of the face, the illusion of the self. I wanted to meditate on the idea that we are all already broken, and in being broken, already whole.

One particular Tibetan lama named Lama Pema (also known as Khenpo Pema Wangdak) visited our rehearsal room at Lincoln Center Theater where we rehearsed the play, and he answered our questions. At one point, Lama Pema leaned forward, laughing, and said, "Art and religion aren't very different. And someone has to do it."

It was not only what Lama Pema told me, it was the presence he evinced—undefinable, not sermonizing but kind, calm, and, yes, happy—that changed me.

I remember being confused about the difference between prayer and meditation until Lama Pema told me it was essentially the same thing. And that the five world religions were essentially the five fingers of the same hand pointing to the same moon.

* * *

After the run of the *The Oldest Boy* was over, I took refuge with an extraordinary Buddhist nun named Jetsunma Tenzin Palmo, who spent nineteen years meditating in a cave in the Himalayas. Refuge essentially means accepting the basic precepts of Buddhism—and I've always loved that it's called refuge rather than conversion—a temporary shelter in belief.

The Buddhist nun said to me, "Are you happy to cut your hair?"

"Yes, I am happy to cut my hair," I said.

And she took a small clipping of my hair.

And then she snapped her fingers, making it so.

CHAPTER 24

I Can Only Imagine

As a child, I saw my father cry only once. We were sitting at a restaurant called the Pancake House out of another time—a time of stained glass, large fluffy Dutch pancakes, and sticks of butter folded into everything. My father and I went once a week to eat pancakes on Saturdays, holy churchless mornings. He taught me a new word every week. *Peripatetic. Defunct. Ostracize.* He told me a story along with the word, so I could remember it.

For example, *ostracize*, from the Greek, spoke of white pieces of pottery on which people voted out offending community members. *Ostracize* was particularly useful to me, thinking of the mean girls at my school.

One time, my father cried at the Pancake House; he was talking about his father. "He was a very gentle man," my father said simply. My father too was gentle—it was perhaps his gentleness that made him notice his father's gentle manner. The ungentle don't tend to notice and praise the gentleness of others.

Before I was born, my father's father died in a duck blind, of a heart attack, in the middle of hunting down ducks, on a river in southern Illinois. My father didn't much care for duck hunting. "It was hard for me to kill the poor little ducks," he said, "but you get caught up in the fervor of it. It was a time for me to be with my dad, for him to be with me. We didn't say much, but we liked sitting in the silence together."

*   *   *

My father never knew I became a playwright, never met my kids. Never met my husband. I dreamed once that he met my husband—I introduced them to each other, in my dream. They enjoyed each other's company.

I spoke to a theater colleague recently who had been through hell when her baby granddaughter died. She said she was disappointed with some acquaintances who kept saying, "I cannot imagine what you are going through." My colleague said she thought, "Well, you could *try*. You could try to imagine. You could at least say: *I can only imagine* what you are going through." This felt like an important moral distinction.

I can only imagine.

I remember when my father was diagnosed with cancer, he went from being a healthy, athletic fifty-two-year-old to an invalid in a matter of days.

One day, my mother was pushing him in his wheelchair down the block in front of our house. His hair was gone from the chemotherapy. Suddenly, he cried out in pain when they went over a small bump in the sidewalk. His back pain was so excruciating that even a tiny crevice in the sidewalk felt monumental. Realizing that there were many such bumps in the sidewalk down the length of our block, my mother gingerly turned the wheelchair around and they went back home.

A neighbor who saw them walking home said later to my mom, "I don't know how you're doing it. You're so brave. *I cannot imagine* what you're going through."

My mom said matter-of-factly that she didn't feel brave, or deserving of pity, she was inside her life—doing what she wanted to be doing—taking care of my father. And it was a nice day, so she was simply taking my father for a walk. My neighbor's polite expression of empathy was, in a way, a negation of the experience of being inside illness. A boundary that many people do not wish to cross.

But don't we need to cross over? Is this not a moral imperative for art, but also for social discourse? Don't we need to imagine people different from ourselves, people whose experiences we can only imagine?

One day, on one of my investigations into the benefits of chiropractics for Bell's palsy, I brought William with me to my appointment. The chiropractor, a compassionate man, with twinkling eyes and a firm, gentle touch, told me that his son was about William's age and showed us pictures of his boy and a bubble machine. I remember vividly the look of joy on his son's face as he reached for a very large bubble.

A month later, I was reading the *Daily News* and saw that a woman had leaped to her death from a ledge on a high-rise building with her five-year-old son. Both died. She was in a custody dispute with her ex-husband, a chiropractor. To punish him, she'd jumped to her death with their child. A high-flying Medea. I looked more closely at the article. This was my chiropractor.

I can only imagine.

That same week, Tony and I and the kids were at a sushi restaurant in Brooklyn, the television on in the corner. The evening news came on. A therapist had been stabbed, murdered in the basement of his Brooklyn house by a stranger. The stranger was apparently lying in wait to rape the therapist's daughter, who escaped. My husband's face went still. "That was my therapist," he said.

"No," I said.

"Yes."

Our kids were watching us, and there was no ritual for this, for seeing on television that someone who profoundly cared for you had been murdered by a stranger. We finished the meal in silence.

I can only imagine.

Bad news comes in threes, so I worried that week about other caretakers. Should I tell Zoe, the acupuncturist, not to leave her apartment? Danger and suffering, everywhere.

One day, commuting to teach in New Haven, I was standing in Penn Station, reading Thomas Merton, when I noticed a monk in saffron robes. It was, in fact, Lama Pema, the Tibetan monk who had visited our rehearsal rooms at Lincoln Center.

We were happy to see each other, and we rode together from New York to New Haven. He looked at my book and was happy, and not the least bit surprised, to see the handwriting of his Tibetan teacher reproduced in Merton's Asian journal. We sat across from each other on the train, and I could not turn from his gaze, so direct and present it was. Lama Pema naturally turned small talk into dharma talk, and said to me over and over, not necessarily knowing about my Bell's palsy but possibly observing it: "You can always choose to smile, no matter what. It is always a choice to smile."

This felt so different from being instructed to smile. It was not a directive, it was a summoning.

In the Zen tradition, one transmission of enlightenment came from the Buddha directly to one of his students through a smile. The Buddha was with his disciples, picked a flower, and quietly held it up. The student, understanding the meaning of the flower, smiled—and so it is said that the teaching came straight through the smile.

There is also a concept in Buddhism of coming to know, through meditation, your original face.

The phrase *original face* comes from the Platform Sutra that asks, "When you're not thinking of anything good and anything bad, at that moment, what is your original face?" The original face is unconditioned, nondualistic, not thinking of good and bad things. It is also something of a paradox, a koan, as in this Zen question: "What was your original face, the face you had before your parents were born?" How can we possibly know what our faces looked like before our own parents were born? Which might lead us to the thought: what we think of as the visible self is not the self at all. This kind of thinking is so different from a dualism that divides a face into a good side and a bad side.

The thirteenth-century Chinese Zen master Mumon wrote of the original face (also translated at times as the true self, or the primal face):

It can't be described! It can't be pictured!
It can't be sufficiently praised! Stop trying to grasp it with
    your head!
There is nowhere to hide the primal face;
Even when the world is destroyed, it is indestructible.

I had been so occupied looking for my *old* face, it hadn't even occurred to me to look for my *original* face.

When I was in my late twenties and living in California, I went to an acupuncture clinic for various health issues. My hair was falling out in clumps, for one thing. (I would learn later that the hair loss was caused by another autoimmune condition called Hashimoto's disease.) The clinic was cheap because acupuncturists in training did the treatments, supervised by their teachers.

One day a Korean master of facial acupuncture and physiognomy came to teach.

He studied my face for a moment, then said, "All I see in your face is father, father, father." He asked what my father did for a living.

I said, "He sold toys."

The acupuncturist heard the past tense. "Ah, I see, your father is dead. Lie down on the table. You have to let go of your father."

No, I thought. No fucking way! I will not let go of my father, or my grief, which is dear to me because my father is dear!

He stuck a needle near my heart and I cried. Not polite crying. Big wracking sobs. The acupuncturist took the needle out gently, and told me to meditate every day for forty days, in order to let my father go.

In the Buddhist schema, the soul wanders for forty days before it finds a new body. Those forty days are crucial for mourners—they must put out food for the wandering soul, pray, and try not to look too grief-stricken, so the departed soul doesn't feel attached to this world.

So, a decade after I lost him, I meditated every day for forty days to let my father go.

CHAPTER 25

Lizard Eye, or Kill the Ingenue

Imagine time passing. The time is marked by about four different new iPhone technologies and four new plays written. In other words, six years pass. Six years of writing, mothering, being.

And all this time—my writing life continued. It may sound like I was in a tunnel of doctor appointments and encounters with Reiki healers—and I was, in part—but I also wrote plays and put them on about once a year. I kept busy. I picked up my children from school. I went to auditions, design meetings. I combed lice out of my children's hair or took them to the lice lady. I took the children to karate, to violin, to the ophthalmologist. I taught. I wrote essays. I worked on a new musical. A new film. Talked on panels. Gave speeches.

For my fortieth birthday, Tony blindfolded me and took me to a flower shop in Brooklyn where he'd made an appointment for us to build terrariums together. We built small green worlds, domed in glass, put light green next to dark green; we made two worlds that could grow, without needing too much water.

As the twins grew, their closeness with each other, their sublime ability to play with each other, meant they needed less supervision than most kids their age, not more. My hypervigilance for their physical well-being transformed into a love of having them on my lap at the library, reading together. They were old enough to *vacuum*. I now had a shocking, luxurious six hours a day to write while all three children were at school. My friends say they saw me then as doing well, not aware of any private anguish. I went to my weekly acupuncture appointments, yes, but I had decided to concern myself with living over and above healing.

After that fateful opening night of *In the Next Room, or the vibrator play*, over the next decade, I put on six more plays and wrote one book of essays. I cowrote a book with my beloved student Max Ritvo. I wrote a new play about my mother as Peter Pan. She grew up playing Peter Pan at the local theater in Davenport, Iowa; once Mary Martin even came through town and my mother got to meet her in the dressing room, as evidenced by the local paper:

Peter Pan Meets Peter Pan As Mary Martin Stops in Town
by Kathy Kehoe

I also wrote new plays about polyamory, and about political dynasties. I served on committees and tried to help other women writers in particular, and tried to help set up funds for childcare for women in the theater. I wrote the libretto for an opera.

A lot of my writing was oral—making up stories for my children at bedtime, which I called Boat of Dreams. I would place all of us in a boat, and adventures would ensue: fairies with broken wings, talking potatoes, talking dolphins—I can't remember any of the stories, so drowsy I was when I told them. I would invent half a story and tell the children to dream the rest, the story a boat to ferry everyone to sleep. . . . I was often the first one to fall asleep.

None of the plays I made during that time, after *In the Next Room*, was as outwardly successful as the work that came before. None came to Broadway, for example. Wrong place at the wrong time, maybe. The quibbles of critics, maybe. But in my mind there grew a soft dividing line between my old life and my new life. A strange and unhelpful metaphor started to take hold that went something like this: after my body got broken by motherhood, the plays were received differently, and, in my imagination, it was all related to my face. Milan Kundera says in *The Unbearable Lightness of Being*: "Metaphors are dangerous. Metaphors are not to be trifled with." Metaphors beget reality.

I began to think: there was a time when the world and I were in harmony, and a time after, and my face was the dividing line. I tried to argue with myself: Your luck has nothing to do with your face. Luck is luck, theater is a fickle mistress, and theater is not the only vocation that favors the young.

I remember the time when I introduced Edward Albee at a PEN America gathering. He had just broken a shoulder riding his motorcycle (in his seventies) and asked me to help him get his leather jacket off. I did. I tried to help him with the other side of his jacket and he stopped me, growling, "I only need help with my broken side."

Onstage, he thanked me for my introduction, and said it was a pleasure to be onstage with such a "young and pretty" playwright. I was still in my thirties. At first I thought: how nice, Edward Albee thinks I'm young and pretty. It was only once I got home that I felt my anger. Why did he comment on my attractiveness, I thought, before a crowd of people who cared about writing and human rights around the world? Why did he erase the fact that I was a writer of some stature with a comment about my youth and desirability? I decided that perhaps his eminence and seniority required an ingenue—defined as artless, unsophisticated, innocent—for a foil.

And that made me want to kill my inner ingenue. And also the writer who wrote ingenues—plays about women in their twenties who were finding love, discarding love, coming into being. Leo, a character from *In the Next Room*, tells Mrs. Givings: "A girl, a woman who is two-thirds done, is nearer to God. A young woman on the verge of knowing herself is the most attractive thing on this earth to a man for this very reason." The audience does not quite trust Leo the artist, for Leo is not very trustworthy.

After *In the Next Room*, I decided it was time to stop writing ingenues. A wild ambition started to take root: to write a play for every decade in a woman's life. A play for an actress at the center in her teens, then twenties, thirties, forties, fifties, sixties, seventies, eighties—I could put the plays in a little box set, take care of these women from the cradle to the grave.

If motherhood breaks you in half, I thought, you must put yourself back together.   .

Then one day, the new iPhone came out with facial recognition technology, and I had to record my face on it. I couldn't quite figure out how, so my husband gently painted my face with my phone in the air. Forced to look at my own face for two minutes in the phone camera, I noticed that my left lip was subtly hitched up all the time so I had a kind of perpetual sneer, while my left eye was drawn down, looking exhausted. Oh, no! I thought. I have what they call resting bitch face. (Obviously RBF is a condition only women can have.)

I read that the playwright Wendy Wasserstein had Bell's palsy too after giving birth to her child. You can see the contrast in the photographs of her before and after giving birth; she had a flashy wide signature grin in her prime. (She also had an outrageous laugh, which I heard in person two times in my life when I met her.) In photos after the birth of her child, she looks either subdued or exhausted. I now recognize that those photos are not of a woman who has lost her joy, or settled into literary gravitas, but instead reveal the face of a woman trying to hide her asymmetry.

I wish I could talk to her about this—about being a playwright and also a mother, about having a subdued half smile after being known for her iconic grin—about how to maintain duration and longevity in a field that often rewards the one-off rather than the long haul—and about the desire to kill off one's inner ingenue.

After nine years of Bell's palsy, it was starting to become clear to me that the reason my face was still crooked when I smiled was not only the unfinished nerve growth, but that I had synkinesis: that pesky Greek word that I avoided learning when the neurologist with the abominable bedside manner told it to me.

What a writerly position I took—if I did not learn the word, I could not have the diagnosis. Synkinesis is when an involuntary muscle movement accompanies a voluntary one; so if you voluntarily smile, you also involuntarily squint. In my case, if I raised my eyebrows, the whole left side of my mouth contorted upwards. If I tried to smile with teeth, my left eye closed, and my neck muscles popped out with effort.

Here I was then at someone else's opening night party. You can see that my left side is making a little attempt at smiling, lips closed, though the left eye squints in protest and my chin reacts in kind.

Humans have bilateral symmetry. Our symmetry helps us recognize each other; and when our symmetry is off, it can be indicative of health concerns.

If a mouth is a bird with two wings, a single wing flapping up signifies effort and brokenness, not beauty or flight. And that is how my smile felt. When you see a bird flap one wing you think: poor bird.

Recently, I was talking to my children at the dinner table about the prospect of writing about Bell's palsy. My son laughed, saying, "You could call the book twisty mouth. Or lizard eye."

"Lizard eye? What's lizard eye?" I asked, confused.

William said, "You always call your left eye your lizard eye when you have to smile for pictures."

"Oh!" I said. "Little eye! My little eye."

I call my left eye "little eye" because whenever I smile, it crumples up, becoming much smaller than my other eye. This is the nature of synkinesis, I now know, since I've bothered to learn the word.

But all this time my son thought I was claiming to have a lizard eye. It makes sense. Lizard eyelids are immobile. And dry.

I did some research and learned that the treatment for synkinesis is limited to biofeedback techniques, experimental surgery, and . . . wait for it . . . *mime therapy*! Yes, mime! Why did I not know this before? Why did the neurologist with the bad bedside manner not tell a playwright, for God's sake, that she could take mime lessons to get better! Did he not realize I would immediately do mime therapy to prevent deterioration of my face, but I would be very unlikely to subject myself to brain surgery? As a theater maker, of course I would love to practice a method created by a mime in the Netherlands. I thought: I will investigate mime therapy. Tomorrow I will find my mime. Where is he? Surely he is in Montmartre wearing red satin suspenders and not in a physical therapy office that takes Aetna.

It finally occurred to me to call my old friend Julie, a neurologist in Rhode Island, to see what she said about synkinesis, and to see if she thought I should investigate experimental surgery rather than mime therapy.

In retrospect, I'm not sure why on earth I didn't call my friend Julie immediately after my diagnosis to ask her detailed questions about my condition. It probably had something to do with shame and not wanting to bother people, and also not wanting a friend to have to give me bad news, like: you will never recover from this. That seemed an odd position to put a friend in.

Julie and I have a lot in common; we both have spontaneous twins and a singleton. She is the only scientist I know who also plays the upright bass in a rock band, paints, and writes detective novels on the side. As such, she can explain scientific things to me using metaphor in a way that few people can.

I called her and asked about my synkinesis, about why a nerve would grow back the wrong way, and why I couldn't just tell my brain to make it grow back the right way? And she said that she wished we could just tell our peripheral nerves where to grow, but they need the scaffolding, which is like a road map to follow. She used the metaphor of cross-country skiing: if someone else's tracks are already there, your skis will just naturally follow those tracks. You don't need to know where the trail is going; you will end up back at the lodge. But if you don't have tracks to follow and you don't know where the trail is, you just kind of wander off and never get to the lodge.

Julie also told me that neurologists historically have been men, and everyone is afraid to do medical studies on pregnant women; and ob-gyns tend to know less about neurology, and as a result, we know very little about neurological disorders that affect women during or right after pregnancy. Now that there are more women neurologists, more studies are being done on the intersection of obstetrics and neurology.

I also asked Julie why I still get weird little electrical sensations on the left side of my face. I'd never asked a doctor before because I wanted to keep the sensation a part of my hopeful imagination, that these sensations were nerve regrowth or reinnervation of the muscle. I didn't want a doctor to tell me the sensations were a stumpy nerve, a twitch, a pathology. Julie told me that both options were possible; that when some branches regrow in brain or spine injuries, people can start getting pain (sometimes six months after an accident), which is the cell trying to regrow its axons.

I asked her about mime therapy. She said she hadn't heard of it, but, why not?

Finally, I asked her if she thought I should get experimental neurosurgery. She said no—that the surgery takes a nerve that is supposed to go to the jaw (a branch of cranial nerve five), splits it, and redirects it to a muscle in the cheek (which is supposed to be supplied by cranial nerve seven, now not functioning perfectly) to make the smile more symmetrical. It's like planting a seed, and it would take months for the procedure to take root and I would only start to see improvement six months after the surgery, that is, if the surgery worked at all. At the moment, apparently there's only a 60 to 85 percent success rate for the surgery (not 60 to 85 percent improvement in nerve function, but a 60 to 85 percent chance that the surgery would work at all).

Forget experimental neurosurgery.

Forget being an ingenue—taking the position of willful unknowing.

And thank God for old friends.

CHAPTER 26

Hermione, the Frozen Statue

When the twins were nine, I went to see *The Winter's Tale* at Theater for a New Audience in Brooklyn, where I was invited to speak on a panel afterwards. As I watched the play, I was struck anew by the frozen statue of Hermione. It is one of the weirder scenes in Shakespeare. We thought Hermione was dead, but now she appears to be a statue, and the statue is about to wake up. Her husband approaches his wife's frozen likeness and remarks: "The very life seems warm upon her lip. / The fixture of her eye has motion in't, / As we are mock'd with art."

Why would a woman get frozen for over a decade, and somehow unfreeze? This question, of course, felt personal to me, as I was still grappling with these questions: When should one simply accept a diagnosis, rather than trying to get better? What is the difference between acceptance and resignation? Is acceptance saying, I take my life, my body as they are? Where, how, does grace enter in?

And I wondered, as I watched *The Winter's Tale*: Is Hermione meant to be a real woman or just a metaphor for art? Is it significant that the *daughter* gazes upon "The statue of her mother"? It is not the husband who wakes the wife, but the woman's friend, Paulina, who says to the statue: "Music, awake her; strike! . . . / 'Tis time; descend; be stone no more. . . . / Bequeath to Death your numbness. . . . / Dear life redeems you. You perceive she stirs."

Be stone no more . . .
She stirs . . .
I thought: someday I will melt.
Someday I will wake up.

Not long after my diagnosis, I had read a moving essay called "Give Me a Smile" in the *New Yorker* by Jonathan Kalb (the very same dramaturge who had invited me to speak about *The Winter's Tale*) about his experience with intractable Bell's palsy. He wrote in the essay about experiencing dampened joy without the accompanying spontaneous physical expression. He wrote about the difficulties of meeting new people—detailing the lengths he went to at parties to speak in profile so that new acquaintances didn't ascribe mal-intent to him.

When I first read Jonathan's essay, sent to me by a playwright friend who knew him, I lightly skimmed it because it was too close to my own experience and too painful to read deeply. Since Jonathan, like me, was one of the minority of Bell's palsy sufferers who never quite recovers, his tale depressed me.

I had always wondered if the diagnosis of chronic Bell's palsy would be any easier if I were a man. Our culture surely likes women to smile, even when they are in pain. Years after reading his essay, I decided, what the hell, I'll ask Jonathan out to lunch. I'll ask him if it's any easier to be a man with Bell's palsy.

We met at the Radiance tea shop. Though I'd never met Jonathan, I recognized him immediately because his face matched mine. We talked, and ate soup. I could feel my mirror neurons firing, looking into the face of someone whose face had experienced what I had, and looking into the eyes of someone who may have felt the same strange disassociation between face and emotion. The empathy I had for Jonathan was boundless. I could see what looked like a flicker of shame on his face when he turned away from me while he laughed. I thought, No, your laugh is beautiful; look at me while you laugh.

I remembered that, in his essay, he wrote that laughter might be the way out of the peculiar depression that the biologically unsmiling have—he pointed out that you don't necessarily need to smile in order to laugh. At lunch, he ate a dumpling that exploded, and he apologized. I told him not to apologize—it can be difficult to eat with Bell's palsy. I tried with difficulty to insert a large cucumber with my chopsticks into my askew mouth, and for once, I didn't feel self-conscious eating with a new acquaintance.

Jonathan told me that he too dreamed of his old face. He too drew an internal line between his life before and after the palsy. He too tried to make his affect into a deadpan version of himself to match his face for a time, then decided to stop doing that. He referred to this as a kind of "coming out." He said that in being willing to reveal himself, he would be attempting to manifest feelings on his face, even if those emotions might look wrong or ugly. Jonathan said several surgeons had contacted him after his article telling him to have surgery, but the surgeries were so experimental and so often worsened the condition that he opted not to.

I finally asked Jonathan what I'd been wondering: if he thought it was any easier for a man to have unrecovered Bell's palsy than for a woman. Jonathan said, "God, yes, at least I think so. I don't want to speak for all women. But it seems to me that women are expected to smile through virtually every difficult situation. Men are allowed to look impassive and serious."

"Well, goddammit," I said. "That's probably true."

At the end of our lunch, Jonathan told me about a neurosurgeon who had some success injecting Botox into the patient's neck to prevent synkinesis; not the experimental surgery I'd heard about in the past, but instead a minimally invasive procedure. Jonathan said the procedure made him feel better for a couple of months and prevented extreme synkinesis, but then he didn't want to have anything more to do with injections. He gave me the neurosurgeon's number, and we said goodbye.

After we parted, I realized that meeting Jonathan gave me, for the first time in nine years, compassion for my own face.

I once saw a talk given by His Holiness the Dalai Lama about how surprised he was by the self-loathing he encountered in the West. He said that in the West, he had to go further than teaching compassion for others; first, he had to teach compassion for the self. In my slow and incomplete recovery from Bell's palsy, I often had more compassion for others with asymmetries than I did for myself. Why? Does one's own face seem like the center of one's will, and therefore worthy of self-blame for not fixing itself?

A week after my lunch with Jonathan, I received a book in the mail from him. He'd written an inscription on the flyleaf from Shakespeare's *Twelfth Night*. It said:

"Methinks 'tis time to smile again."

CHAPTER 27

The Neurosurgeon Who Liked Irishwomen

The neurosurgeon's office was on the Upper East Side. (The location worried me a little, as it had been the land of bad news for me, but I still made the trek.) While waiting in the office foyer, I scrolled on my phone through some studies on Bell's palsy and depression. One study made me laugh because its conclusions seemed so obvious:

"A significant proportion of participants with facial palsy, experience psychological distress as a result of their condition. . . ."

Ah, yes.

"Other research shows that females report greater psychological distress, possibly owing to the greater emphasis placed on their appearance by society. . . ."

Check.

"Female participants had significantly higher levels of anxiety compared with male participants. Female and male participants were equally likely to experience high levels of depression."

Yup. And:

"These studies have demonstrated that there is no direct relationship between the objective degree of disfigurement and the subjective degree of distress experienced."

Huh. Yes. And:

"It has been noted that it is the inability to smile and express emotion that is most distressing to facial palsy patients."

But I knew that already.

The neurosurgeon called me in.

The doctor sat me down across from a formidable oak desk to take my history. The first thing out of his mouth was, "You're very pretty." I decided this must be his usual way to disarm his disfigured patients. He took a good lengthy history, paying close attention and writing things down. Again, I told my anecdote about the lactation consultant who said my eye was droopy, and how I had joked, "I'm Irish."

He looked up, "You're Irish?" He looked intrigued.

"Yup," I said. I wondered if he too would make the celiac connection.

Instead he said, "I have a weakness for Irishwomen. Very beautiful. An Irishwoman was once the love of my life." I somehow divined that the Irishwoman was not his wife; sure enough, he let slip that he was recently divorced.

He returned to the business at hand, telling me he could do a cross-facial nerve graft, taking muscles from my leg and attaching them to my face, but that I'd need to relearn to smile by clenching a different facial muscle. "Well, doesn't that sort of defeat the purpose?" I asked. "Isn't the whole point to feel what it's like to have a spontaneous smile again?"

"I see your point," he said, "but let's go into the examining room and see what's what."

In the exam room, he sat me down and took up residence on a little rolling stool, spreading his legs. He started measuring my face. He scooted his little rolling stool between my knees so that our knees touched. Well, I thought, he has to get in there close to measure my face. He gave measurements to the nurse who stood in back, taking down numbers. He looked closely at my face, a medical gaze, or something else? Both? I couldn't tell. He put metal instruments into my mouth and bid me bite down, then smile. The nurse took pictures of me trying to smile with metal instruments in my mouth. Then we went back into his office.

He sat behind his desk. "As I said, you're a good-looking woman." I scrunched myself lower into my chair. I'd never been told I was a good-looking woman that many times in an hour and it was starting to make me feel creepy. In fact, I don't think anyone had called me a "good-looking woman" to my face before. It reminded me mainly that I was a woman. I continued to hope that all this flattery was a medical therapeutic strategy.

"Now, look," he said, "I'll help you because I like you, and I don't like everyone, and when you're my age you say what you think. You're charming."

"Thank you," I said, thinking, Wouldn't he help me because he's a doctor and I'm paying him?

But he went on: "So, I could do the surgery, and we can use the exogenous muscles to transfer to the mouth. I'm an excellent surgeon, so it would go well." Then he gestured to some awards he had on his wall, for doing complicated neurosurgery on children with brain tumors, and told me that he had saved many lives. "But," he said, "you're the mother of three, and it's a serious surgery, and I'm not sure you want to go through that." I nodded in agreement.

"Instead, I'm going to recommend Botox for the synkinesis; it's a much less invasive procedure." He explained that the Botox would freeze the good side of my face to match the bad side. And he could also temporarily paralyze the muscles that the left side was incorrectly recruiting to do its work. I thought: Why would I want to paralyze the side of my face that is lucky enough to have the joy of motion intact? I wanted more mobility, more expression, and he wanted to paralyze even more of my face for symmetry's sake. He went on: "It's medical Botox, so it'll be covered by insurance." He cautioned: "It's tricky to strike a balance between helping the resting face become symmetrical in repose, and the animated face while making an expression. You help one, and you hurt the other, and vice versa."

He leaned forward and looked at me intently. "So," he said, "it would have to be a collaboration."

"A collaboration?" I asked. I'm used to collaboration—I work in the theater.

"You'd have to come back frequently to tell me how you like it. It would require us to date, if you will."

Stunned, I wrote down his words in my little notebook. In his mind, would he sculpt me, an Irish Pygmalion, then throw me on a couch in the waiting room? "You don't have to write that all down," he said. Oh yes I do, I thought. He went on: "I'll take care of everything; we'll get you preapproved for medical Botox. Of course, prices are going up because of Obamacare . . . and illegal aliens. . . ." Good Lord, I thought. Is he really going *there*? I got up to leave. He touched my elbow as I left the room. I fled.

The next day the nurse called to say that my insurance had indeed preapproved me for medical Botox. "No, thank you," I said. She seemed surprised. There was no way I would let that man touch my face.

I thought: Like it or not, I'm going to die with this face. I may as well fall in love with it.

CHAPTER 28

The Good Doctor and Gratitude

It strikes me that the difference between a good doctor and a less-than-good doctor is one part expertise and three parts quality of listening. When I joked about my Irish ancestry to Russell Chin, he had a clinical instinct to check for celiac disease. When I joked about my Irish ancestry to the unnamed neurosurgeon, he reflected on his amorous taste for Irishwomen.

I am married to a good doctor. I imagine he listens to his patients with the same calm empathy with which he listens to me and to our children. I remember when he took his medical school's updated version of the Hippocratic oath, and I felt slightly worried when he had to swear to care about his patients as much as his family.

Now, when I look up the traditional Hippocratic oath, I see no reference to this promise. Did I exaggerate at the time, worried about my own potential displacement in a hierarchy of needs? And did this worry come from my grandmother, also a doctor's wife but when that meant a very different thing, in the 1950s in small-town Iowa? My grandfather, too, was a good doctor, going from house to house with his brown medical bag. He was rarely home, but he saved the lives of many children, and worked tirelessly on the Salk polio vaccine trials.

* * *

In the time of the pandemic, the good doctor is everywhere. The good doctor shows up despite crushing exhaustion, lack of supplies, possible contagion, death, and harm to self and family. My parsing of the good and less-than-good doctor—the doctor who listens exceptionally well versus one who doesn't—seems to belong to an antiquated, privileged past, a time before extremity. A time when we were justified in complaining about this and that. A time before the heroism of the medical profession was what might save us all.

Even when patients cannot speak—the good doctor is still listening to the patient's body, still observing, through a mask.

I once asked Julie—one of the heroic good doctors—how she empathizes with patients when they're at the end of the line, no more treatments available, or when they're dealing with a neurological loss that is intimately related to their identity. She told me that for really tough cases, she sometimes has patients make a list of things they are grateful for—not the generic things people always list at Thanksgiving by rote like "I'm grateful for my friends and family" but all the specific things you rely on in life—and then imagine if you don't put every specific thing on the list, they might disappear by midnight.

I start thinking of my list:

I am grateful that my husband's heart is beating.
I am grateful for hot showers.
I am grateful for my children's limbs.
I am grateful for my children's minds.
I am grateful that my children still allow me to cuddle
    with them before bed.
I am grateful that I can go to the grocery store.
I am grateful for my hair.

I am grateful for my bed.

I am grateful for my dog. And for the fact that her tail
   was not cut off in the elevator that time it got stuck in
   the door.

I am grateful for a cool glass of water that I can get from
   the tap.

I am grateful there is no leak in my ceiling.

And as I write these words, I suddenly ache for any reader who
may need the things I am grateful for—and I am self-conscious,
boasting of my plenty.

And I stop writing my list.

And yet, knowing that we all have different, incomprehensible
losses, and different kinds of plenty, I keep writing.

I am grateful that my fingers work.

I am grateful to be able to smell and taste soup.

I am grateful for my mother's laugh.

I am grateful that my sister tells it like it is.

I am grateful that I can afford to buy new underwear
   when my dog chews up my old underwear.

I am grateful to be alive.

I could go on . . . and on . . . and on . . . and on. . . .

Suddenly my half-smile problem seems so small, so very
small. . . .

I am grateful for the friend who brought me blueberries.

I am grateful for the friend who brought me a car seat.

I am grateful I can write the word *grateful.*

A prayer starts to form in my mind:

Let me be grateful, and let me be of use.

CHAPTER 29

Ding-Dong, Ding-Dong,
or Grow Accustomed to Your Face

Here is the poet Allen Ginsberg, above, with Bell's palsy.

Ginsberg, the author of *Howl*, was mistakenly told he had had a stroke for years when it was actually incurable Bell's palsy. The phrase *ding-dong*, a doctor once told me, is a mnemonic device for medical students to remember a Bell's palsy diagnosis when they might falsely diagnose stroke. ("Ding-dong"—bell—get it?) If a medical student sees a droopy face while rounding, they might alert a fellow intern with a cheerful: "Ding-dong." Ding-dong, ding-dong, howl.

I am struck in this photograph by how Ginsberg is not hiding from his facial anomaly. There is no attempt to shift to the side, put a hand over a cheek, or change the lighting. Plus, he's clean-shaven, though he often sported a long beard. That's one tool a man has that a woman doesn't have to hide Bell's palsy—grow a beard.

I am a poet and this is my face, the photograph seems to be saying.

Having decided not to hide my face, or hide *from* my face any-more, I searched for a physical therapist, ten years after diag-nosis. I couldn't find mime therapy in New York, but I did find a physical therapist online who specialized in Bell's palsy. It was my first trip to a physical therapist since having my picture taken by some gym buffoon while I looked like Cosmo in *Singin' in the Rain*. I had never gone back.

But I had been learning about neuroplasticity, and thought it might be worth a try. Julie told me that neuroplasticity is es-sentially the idea that your brain can change post-trauma—that, in fact, an old dog *can* learn new tricks. For example, when a neurosurgeon takes out half of a child's brain (yes, this really happens, usually because the child's epilepsy is so severe that it is life-threatening) the child can still learn to talk or relearn to use the arm or leg that the removed hemisphere was responsible for. Julie had two patients who had hemispherectomies (one per-formed by Ben Carson). Both of these patients are doing well—they can talk, walk, communicate. One had a baby.

Apparently, we used to think a brain couldn't grow new cells, but now we know that new cells can actually be born in a part of the brain called the hippocampus. Julie explained that neuro-plasticity is the regrowth of pathways and synapses around the injured parts, making the remaining cells work just a little harder. With peripheral nerves, the cell body lives outside the brain, and when the cell dies, it dies; but if that cell was responsible for making a muscle move, another cell that was only slightly injured can grow a branch, or axon, learning to reinnervate a weak muscle.

I learned about a neuroscientist, Dr. Edward Taub, who made advances with stroke victims with profound learned non-use on one side. He essentially helped reprogram their brains by tying down their good sides and forcing them to use their broken sides. The bad side would be forced to wake up and work when the good side was taped down, or in a sling.

It made sense to me that the same thing could be done on the face. I called to see if the Taub training clinic would take a Bell's palsy patient. The answer was, they don't treat that. I am outside protocol. If I am to engage in the search for this kind of neuroplastic therapy, it will be on my own.

Elaine meets me in a private room. She tells me that she herself has had Bell's palsy three times, and her sister, through a genetic disorder, has had it ten times. Unfortunately, her office is, you guessed it, on the Upper East Side. Elaine, a physical therapist, is about my age, has a small daughter, and is from Morocco by way of Ecuador and the Bronx. She tells me that she'll talk to me all kinds of nonsense and chatter, but it's to a higher purpose: she wants to see what facial expressions I'll make while she talks.

Then she asks me to smile.

I have not allowed someone to look at me, to really look at me, while I tried to smile in a long time. Not my friends. Not my children. Not my own mother. Not even Tony. Allowing this woman, this comparative stranger, to look at me while I try to smile imperfectly feels like its own healing.

Crucially, unlike the physical therapist at the high-end gym, she doesn't ask me to use a mirror. Her face is my mirror, and she makes the expressions along with me. As a result, I can try to make the expressions without feeling shame.

Shame is an odd emotion. It clings to things over which we have no control, like a scent. Rationally, I did not do anything to cause my misshapen face—so why then shame? Is that what original sin (another concept that has never resonated for me) is all about? That, through no fault of our own, we feel marked? I have always understood guilt as a Catholic, although I've never understood organizing world religions around the concept of guilt rather than around the concept of kindness. Guilt was when I stole that Juicy Fruit gum from the convenience store as a four-year-old and felt so guilty I chewed one piece in my closet and threw out the rest.

Shame, on the other hand, has always seemed to me mysterious. Is shame just guilt plus being seen?

They call it "shamefaced"; the face telegraphs shame. Without consciously admitting it, I was ashamed of my face. I was ashamed of the very instrument that is supposed to express shame.

Shame happens when there is the consciousness of the body being seen and simultaneously not being controlled. Shame is the shape of a fig leaf, but you can't put a fig leaf over your face.

Shame is when a group of thirteen-year-old kids dropped me off at my house, and I said good night, went up to my bedroom on the second floor, and changed into my flannel nightgown near a window, not knowing that a girl in the group told the gaggle of kids to stay and watch, because the windows didn't have curtains. When I got to school the next day, I realized the same girl told everyone in school that I purposely got naked in my bedroom, a thirteen-year-old exhibitionist, so that a gaggle of boys could watch. The body was seen without its control or permission.

Shame is when, as a child, I stained my underwear, and was so ashamed that I hid the underwear in a strange little drawer in my bureau, so no one would see it in the laundry. I came upon it years later.

Shame is different from public humiliation. One can feel humiliated without feeling ashamed. Getting a bad review of a play in public, for example, can be humiliating, but it does not necessarily lead to shame.

As a twenty-year-old, I remember going to my pigeonhole for mail when studying in England and finding the word *lesbian* scrawled next to my name. I'd always felt my desire was formed specifically and exclusively in terms of person and not exclusively or specifically in terms of gender, though I may not have had words for that then. Had the writer seen something on my body, on my face, that I did not know I was revealing? Certainly I was not straight like an arrow. Did my outsize crush on my best friend, a woman, in England make it so? Or was the pigeonhole graffiti artist tipped off by all the naked figure drawings taped to the walls of my room, the stacks of Virginia Woolf, or was it the gender-bending twenty-first birthday party where I dressed in trousers, suspenders, and a mustache? Had the writer peered into childhood dreams or into the future? I did not think the word on my mailbox was bad, but the writer must have thought it was bad. I thought the poison-pen writer did not understand my expansive, subtle, and private experience of my own body, but, then again, I wondered: perhaps I was deluded. How could that writer understand me when I didn't quite understand myself? And so I felt what the poison-pen writer wanted me to feel: I felt shame.

Shame leads to blushing. The barometer for visible shame is on the face. The expression *to lose face* comes from a Chinese expression meaning to be disgraced, unable to show one's face in public.

One thing that I have always loved about Tony is that he has never made me feel ashamed.

* * *

Now, mirroring Elaine's expressions, I realize I have had such shame over my broken face that I have not even attempted many subtle expressions for a decade.

There are so many ways to hide. It does not take a genius or a villain to play peekaboo with life. "Show your face!" yells the cowboy to the villain, who is lurking in the shadows, face wreathed in semidarkness, sniveling coward that he is, unwilling to show his self, which is congruent with his face.

"Raise your eyebrows," says Elaine, doing it with me. "Now, grimace." We grimace together. "Look like you're smelling a bad smell." I allow her to take pictures of me doing these expressions, so that she has a baseline for my progress. She calculates on a piece of paper that I'm about 70 percent broken on the left side of my face. Somehow, I still feel hopeful. But when I get on the subway and look at the photos she's taken of my contorted face, and how broken I look, I delete them all and want to die.

One day, Tony and I make breakfast for the kids, while we listen to the radio. An interview with the brilliant actress Lupita Nyong'o comes on NPR. The interviewer asks Lupita about beauty. And about colorism, which caused Lupita, a dark-skinned woman, to feel less than beautiful as a child. She says that one of her mother's maxims was, "You can't eat beauty." You can't eat beauty, how marvelous, I think. The interviewer, a woman, goes on to ask Lupita how it felt to be the most beautiful woman in the world. After denouncing a ridiculous standard of light-skinned beauty, the interviewer puts Lupita back in the beauty box. And back we go, into our boxes.

I lie down on a table and Elaine puts on blue latex gloves and sticks her hands in my mouth. She stretches out the masseter muscle in my cheek. This is painful. There are essentially three muscles controlling the smile and the masseter is one of them, as is the risorius, which Elaine talks to like an old friend. "Come on, risorius," she says. "Now smile," she says. "Smile with teeth." I practice smiling at her.

"One, two, three, smile!" I try to smile with her hand in my mouth. "Oooh," she says, "that smile was so much more spontaneous—could you feel it?" I can't tell; it's hard to know if your smile feels spontaneous when you're told to smile. Still, Elaine is pleased with my progress. "One, two, three, smile!" she proclaims. And I practice smiling. And in practicing smiling, I think: Is smiling a practice? And is joy a muscle?

She continues to stretch my cheek muscles out, her blue-gloved hand pressing inside my mouth. Then she tells me that her father died last week. "I'm so sorry," I try to say, without much ability to speak. She tells me that he was ninety-six and lived a good life. But she says that her own mother weeps and then doesn't weep and then feels guilty that she is not sad all the time. "It's confusing to grieve," I try to say, her hand in my mouth, but it comes out garbled.

After my own father died, my sister and mother and I occupied the same dark house, but our ways of grieving were different, private. I knew we were all sad, but we didn't necessarily cry together. We got a new dog whom we trained, badly. The house was quiet.

I had a vivid dream then that I wrote down: a doctor looked inside my mouth and said, "Ah—I see—I see that inside you are crying! Do you know joy, young lady?"

And I said, "A lady named Joy?"

And he said, "Not the woman, young lady! Joy—joy—joy! Aha! That will be two thousand dollars, young lady. You can pay me in cash, young lady; that will be all, young lady; wear a mask on the way out."

I continue to practice my facial expressions at home in front of the mirror. I do Elaine's exercises for synkinesis, trying to retrain the face not to use the wrong muscles to make an expression. I pucker my lips while lifting my eyebrows. I open my mouth wide. I smile with the help of my finger. I grimace. Like this:

And Elaine tells me that by hook or by crook, I am improving.

When Anna was twelve, I took her to Lincoln Center's production of *My Fair Lady*. We were there to see my friend Laura Benanti, who had played the role of Mrs. Givings in *In the Next Room, or the vibrator play* years ago, take over the role of Eliza. Before the curtain rose, we prowled the same backstage halls where I had rehearsed so many plays, where I had breastfed Anna, where I had been pregnant with the twins.

As we watched the show, I listened with new attention to the song "I've Grown Accustomed to Her Face." I've never liked Henry Higgins much as a character—he's a bit of an asshole—but this actor's rendition of this song was fierce and full of pathos. After congratulating Laura, who was changing out of her nineteenth-century gown while her toddler played in her dressing room, Anna and I walked to the subway. And I whistled to myself the song that starts "Damn, damn, damn, damn!"

I could almost whistle now. My cheeks swerved to the side, and the sound was a little reedy, but still . . . I whistled: *I've grown accustomed to my face . . . like breathing out and breathing in.*

I so badly wanted to be accustomed to my face.

Trial and error. Breathing out and breathing in. Effort might lead to failure or mild improvement. But not trying at all meant not improving at all. I was trying, for the first time in such a long time.

CHAPTER 30

Mirror Neurons and Narcissus

After three months of physical therapy I noticed a profound difference in my face. I had more mobility, and, what's more, I made facial expressions socially that I had studiously avoided for a decade. I realized that part of the therapy in physical therapy was trying to make an expression while looking another person in the face. Could this be an example, I wondered, of those mysterious new things they have discovered in our brains called mirror neurons?

Mirror neurons are brain cells that react when an action is performed or observed. When someone grimaces, we register their pain. When someone yawns, we yawn. When someone smiles, we smile. Some argue that mirror neurons are actually the neurological basis for empathy. The theater is all about mirror neurons; we watch actors feel, and we feel what they are feeling. And apparently mothers teach their babies empathy by mirroring their expressions.

When I first read about mirror neurons, I worried—did I screw up my babies by not being able to sufficiently mirror them? In the burgeoning mirror neuron literature, Marco Iacoboni writes: "Baby smiles, the parent smiles in response. Two minutes later, baby smiles again, the parent smiles again. . . . Therefore—presto! Mirror neurons for a smiling face are born." This magical

feedback loop is well expressed in this picture of me as a baby
smiling at my mother. We are mirroring each other perfectly:

Iacoboni and others theorize that by imitating a smile, or other
facial expressions, not only do we learn to smile, we also come to
understand what the other is thinking and feeling. By imitating,
we come to know and feel empathy. If his suggestion is correct,
my inability to model smiling would not only inhibit the smiles of
my children, it would also inhibit empathy.

My children hate smiling for photographs. Is it my fault?

The mirror I continue to hate most of all is my bathroom mirror.
I avoid it studiously. It's a dual-sided vanity mirror that I never
would have chosen and it has a cruel objectivity capable of eras-
ing all my progress. When opened, the face is reflected, not from
the frontal vantage point where one's perception fills in gaps, but
from a kind of omniscient point of view. This is helpful if you are
trying to see a part of your face that you normally can't see, to
check for a mole, or to see if you braided your hair well.

But it is not helpful if you don't want to see the left side of your smile as it actually is and not how you would like it to be.

There is so much that a mirror, or a camera, cannot see. Neither cameras nor mirrors can see history, memory, love. Cameras fix a moment in time. I think my friends and my husband can see in my face the memory of my old face, and they give me the benefit of the doubt, filling in some measure of intention, some of the old symmetry. They give it to me for free, because of love. At least I imagine that they do.

My mother has, for the last fifteen years, been back together with her high school sweetheart from Davenport, Iowa. They found each other again after both were widowed. To hear them laugh together, it's clear that they still see each other as the sixteen-year-olds they were then, now occupying different bodies.

The image of the self, with its history and intentionality, is enhanced by the imagined gaze of the other. In this day and age, the age of selfies, we are lost in images of ourselves, deprived of the other's gaze.

These images of the self have a sterile hall-of-mirrors quality, an inescapable *narcissism* (a word that is tossed around a lot these days). But who was Narcissus, really?

Narcissus was a boy who fell in love with the boy he saw in a reflection. A boy who loved the image of his own face in the water, without knowing or recognizing himself. But in not knowing that his image was *himself*, can Narcissus really be said to be narcissistic?

We can never truly look back at ourselves. Not in the water, not in a mirror, not with a camera. Our faculties do not permit us to see ourselves with the eyes of another. Is love the purest technology for self-regard?

*　*　*

My husband remarked at some point during my recovery that over the last decade I had become increasingly withdrawn. Was I submerging myself so deeply into the role of an observer that I myself was hardly there? Did I want to take my mind and spirit so far inside that no one would dare associate either with my face? Like a turtle, winnowing back in and down; remove the shell and I would be pure spirit. This is a radical act in the age of selfies. What is true self-regard in the age of narcissism and endless self-reflections?

My dearest friends tell me now they have been completely unaware of this dance of self-erasure I've been doing for the last decade. I kept it all hidden, even from them.

But I couldn't hide it from Tony; he notices too much.

After months of physical therapy, I see the left corner of my mouth creeping up with more intention during a smile. I stop covering my mouth when I laugh.

I try to smile and laugh with people while looking at them in the eye, without turning away. This turning away, this learned impassive stare, this hiding, I now realize, was partly shame but also a kind of deluded caring for the other—I did not want them to feel they had to care for me if they noted my contortion, my effort. I wanted to spare them my asymmetry.

Now, in public places, I find myself smiling at babies who are not my own.

At one café, the most beautiful baby wakes up from a nap. The fullest cheeks. The mother is reading and I smile at this stranger's baby with all the muscular force I could not muster when I was smiling at my twins. Yes, you, baby-who-I-do-not-know, I think, I am smiling at you and you can tell I am smiling and you smile back and that makes me smile more at you, you adorable random stranger baby.

The baby's mother glances up from her work and looks at me.

Is she thinking: Who is the crazy lady maniacally smiling at my baby? Is she about to kidnap him? She picks him up and holds him close.

When I go back to Elaine, she measures my improvement, impressed. And one day, the facial recognition on my phone ceases to recognize me. My own phone doesn't know me. My facial measurements must have changed objectively. What a world. We are known by our phones.

Feeling my progress internally, rather than in the mirror, as access to a more ready smile, I start finding myself smiling at strangers more often. One day, a woman walks towards me on the street. I can see clearly that she has Bell's palsy. The whole side of her face is drawn downward and sideways, pinched. I try to smile at her, try to show her as well as I can with my face, that I understand something of what she is experiencing, and that I wish her happiness in this moment.

She smiles back at me, with the right side of her face.

Elaine tells me that one of her Bell's palsy patients had the strange impression that her eye was an alien. Her eye felt like it belonged to someone else, because the facial muscles around the eye could not move. Her face continued to get better, but still her unblinking lizard eye felt like the eye of an alien. Finally, after months of physical therapy, she said, "I feel like it's my eye again!" And she cried.

Thinking about how therapeutic it is to mirror Elaine's facial expressions at physical therapy, I decide to try my luck mirroring actors in the dark at home, watching videos. Action movies are good for mirroring because the protagonist grimaces in ways I never would normally grimace, stretching my range. Phoebe Waller-Bridge in *Fleabag* is good for ironic expressions—she is a genius at pulling faces. And I sit in the dark, trying to imitate them all.

Marlon Brando's eyebrows tell a thousand tales, and as I watch him raise and lower them, I try my best to do the same. Eyebrows tell stories. If you can't move your eyebrows, it is harder for your face to tell a story. Why, of all animals, are dogs adorable and so human seeming? Dogs, unlike cats, appear to have eyebrows. And therefore, they appear to smile.

My progress is not linear. I practice smiling. In earnest. This involves looking in the mirror. A thing I have avoided for the last decade. It occurs to me now that the refusal of the woman in the mirror was a refusal of embodiment altogether.

After a decade, I allow a friend to photograph me smiling with teeth. I find the image so hideous, I want to erase my face until I am the woman in the Matisse painting *Plum Blossoms, Green Background.*

In the painting, the woman's facial features are erased, so that she has the same status as the objects in the painting. Oh, faceless woman, I think, you whose face has attained the stillness of objects . . . who are you?

There is another faceless woman in this painting by Gustave Moreau. He often painted Helen of Troy without a face. A blank. Was she so beautiful that her face was too beautiful to paint? Or was painting her face a kind of violence, a violence

Helen on the Ramparts of Troy that her face incited?

* * *

When the face is a mask, the soul hides or relocates. I am trying to welcome my soul back into my face. What percent healed
would I need to be in order to accept my face as my face again?
Joy is a deeply embodied emotion. It is floating down a river. It is
watching an acrobat swing in the air, laughing in response. It is
not looking in the mirror.

But now, doing physical therapy, I try to ignore my aesthetic
response and focus instead on objective things like the limits of
my muscles. I focus on reclaiming more elasticity and strength,
rather than on trying to reclaim an idea of beauty. I focus on what
I can *do* with my face, rather than how my face looks. In other
words, I try to prize function, purpose, and intention over vanity
and symmetry. *What I am doing* with the muscles of my face, not
how I am seen.

And I slowly improve, graduating even to practicing my frown.
It can be, apparently, physiologically more difficult to frown than
smile. It involves many more facial muscles; and the muscle on
my chin doesn't want to engage. When I look in the mirror and
try to frown, I feel sensation in the left half of my face, like tiny
windshield wipers in the nerves going back and forth, or like tiny
people pulling a rope across my cheek. I can't tell if it's symp-
tomatic of recovery or damage. It is, in any case, sensation. As I
try to tap the muscles alive, to beckon them into effort—I think
about how fewer muscles are necessary to glide into joy than are
required to furrow one's brow or to crumple one's chin into sadness.

As I close my eyes hard, squint, and blow, a melody from a
Yeats poem goes through my head: "One man loved the pilgrim
soul in you, / And loved the sorrows of your changing face."

* * *

In my pilgrimage, I go to see yet another chiropractor. This one was recommended to me by my choreographer friend who, after she gave birth, couldn't walk. For a dancer, this was devastating. This chiropractor helped her walk again.

This new highly recommended chiropractor has some strange magic. She measures the length of my legs to see if they're even. She says they aren't even. Her touch is very gentle. (My grandfather, a pediatrician from Davenport, Iowa, was suspicious of chiropractors, and Davenport, Iowa, was the birthplace of the chiropractic method. So I have a granddaughter's skepticism, but since I've started to try again, I'll try anything that won't hurt.)

Within one visit to the magical chiropractor, my face seems to be visibly improving. It makes no scientific sense. But the muscles are starting to come alive again. I keep doing the facial exercises Elaine gave me—pursing my lips, squinting, frowning, snarling while looking in the mirror.

At the suggestion of a beloved theater colleague at Yale, I try Alexander Technique too for the hell of it. Alexander Technique is a system of changing posture and reducing tension in the body—particularly the neck and head—that is taught regularly now to actors but also to people who suffer from Parkinson's disease. The technique was created by Frederick Matthias Alexander—a nineteenth-century Shakespearean orator from Tasmania—who lost his voice and created a system of movement to get his voice back. His famous satisfied clients included John Dewey, Aldous Huxley, and George Bernard Shaw.

With my Alexander teacher, I learn a new way of walking and of sitting. I feel like a baby, practicing tasks that should be automatic, like smiling and walking and lying down. I enjoy holding myself in this infantile state. It feels like a form of *doing* rather than *receiving* treatment.

And by hook or by crook, with all of this practice, my smile seems wider, more immediate. My crow's-feet seem to coordinate with my smile, creating the spontaneous Duchenne look.

I go to Elaine again and she tests my facial muscles' mobility, and this time I get a score of only 38 percent disfigured, compared to the 70 percent I walked in with. Does that mean that I should be 62 percent happy? My joy has moved, physically speaking, to the majority. The numbers are now on my side.

Why is physical therapy not routinely recommended for Bell's palsy? Because there is no proven protocol. And insurance companies don't want to pay for unproven techniques. This makes sense—why should people waste time and money on things that do not work? Elaine is to some extent making up the protocol as she goes along; but, in my case, it seems to be slowly working. She's inventing exercises based on her expertise as a physical therapist, and based on her own experience having Bell's palsy. She is joining the long line of medical professionals who experiment on themselves to make discoveries, and I am one of the beneficiaries.

I do my exercises dutifully, aware that the therapy might have less to do with the physical exercises and more to do with allowing myself to be seen.

One week, she has me focus on blowing air in my mouth from side to side. It's surprisingly difficult, and air leaks out the left side like a sad flatulent wind. But I keep at it, and my lips grow stronger, keeping the air in. When I brush my teeth at night, I try moving water from the right side of my mouth to the left, until I can do it without water spurting out at the mirror. Success.

People talk about faces as beautiful or not beautiful, not as strong or weak. We might speak of a feature being strong or weak. "What a weak chin," we might say about a man, in particular. Or we might speak of a nose being strong. Perhaps we think of protrusions as being strong or weak. But we don't say, "What a strong smile." Now I know—it takes muscular strength to smile. The only people I can think of who talk about strong lips are trumpet players.

So, on a whim, I start doing exercises to help what wind and brass musicians call embouchure. I look up videos on YouTube to do at home, like the one with a brisk Englishwoman who barks, "How to care for your floppy face."

One day, for the second time, I swipe up on my phone and my facial recognition software doesn't recognize me. Hmm, I think. My face must be changing. When I see my internal medicine doctor for a checkup, she says, unprompted, that my face looks remarkably better.

And so I start smiling at strangers. It might lead to an addiction, this new smiling at people in line at the grocery store. It might lead to misunderstandings.

On November 19, 2019, I go to Elaine, she watches my expressions, and then she says, write down the date: this is the day your first synkinesis was killed.

What she means is this—whenever I used to raise my eyebrows, post-Bell's, the whole left side of my face contorted to help. Big muscles, more powerful than little muscles, get recruited to do difficult tasks. So for the partially paralyzed, a big muscle conspires to do a job it was not designed to do. For the past eight months doing PT, I have been tricking my face not to contort when I raise my eyebrows.

Elaine is excited. She says the next step is to blow up balloons, which I still can't do. Whenever the twins give me balloons to blow up, I hand them to Anna. But today I buy some shiny green balloons on the way home.

And as I walk, I whistle this tune: *Smile, though your heart is aching . . . Smile, what's the use of crying?*

I get home and pucker up, I blow, I blow, I blow—I can't do it.

Luckily, I think, I'm not a magician—blowing up balloons is not part of my vocation.

I may not be able to blow up balloons, but I have a new, very hard-won smile line on the left side. And I think: lucky the lines on all of our faces. Lucky the laugh lines and the smile lines especially; they signify mobility, duration, and joy.

And I think about how love has many faces. How my husband has loved me and my changing face and body over time. And how, in return, though less dramatically, because the transformation is much subtler, I love his changing face over time. The new white hairs. The wrinkles.

As the Uruguayan poet Amanda Berenguer writes in her long-form ode to wrinkles, "Wrinkles are the straw from which old age builds its nest."

I remember the first time, after my diagnosis, that I smiled without thinking. It was springtime, and a small child wandered towards me, with a red ball. The ball zigzagged towards me, and I tried not to get in its way. An old man watched this dance and smiled at me. I smiled back. Crooked, but impulsive and therefore with joy.

I decide to reoccupy my body—I decide to take up tenancy again.

CHAPTER 31

The Fortune Cookie

A decade ago, I got a fortune cookie that said, "Deliver what is inside you, and it will save your life." At the time, I thought the fortune might simply mean: If you don't deliver these babies in a timely fashion, they will kill you.

But what if it meant something else?

This past Christmas, I was at my mother's apartment in Evanston, Illinois, and on a mission to learn something about a particular Irish ancestor. My great-great-great-grandfather Patrick Gregg fought on the side of the North in the Civil War, was captured in the South, and wrote scurrilous verse about his Southern captors and threw his verses outside his jail window for publication. I felt an ancestral curiosity about this man. I was paging through photo albums and old, yellowed documents, looking for his verses, when I came upon my father's dark brown leather baby book, full of his mother's handwriting. I opened it and came upon a page that read:

Pat Ruhl: Pyloric spasms when a baby. Could not eat any food except banana and milk until two years old. Believe it is called "celiac disease."

I put down the baby book, stunned.

My father never knew he had celiac disease as a baby. We now know that celiac disease is not a pediatric illness that we outgrow but an immunological response that is lifelong and, if left untreated, dramatically increases your risk of all kinds of other diseases, including cancer. Three kinds of cancer are associated with celiac disease; one is adenocarcinoma, the rare cancer that my father had.

When he was the age I am now, my father started having all kinds of physical problems: including peripheral neuropathy, tingling in hands and feet, sciatic nerve pain, unbearable back pain. The doctors couldn't explain it. He was hospitalized; they did all kinds of tests. He was put on painkillers, then steroids. He was a little manic, and enraged, on steroids. He smoked cigars from his bed, going through his address book, calling friends all night. My father had never smoked a cigar in his life to my knowledge, and now he was wreathed in smoke. A famed Chicago doctor, notorious for his lack of bedside manner and his extraordinary diagnostic powers, finally diagnosed the mystery disease. Pernicious anemia. My father would inject himself with B_{12} vitamins monthly, thinking himself cured. We didn't know it then, but the famed diagnostician was most likely treating only symptoms.

My father died of cancer when he was fifty-four. If he'd known he'd had celiac disease, and treated it, who knows? He might have avoided cancer and lived to meet his grandchildren.

When he was fifty-two, my father and my sister and my mother drove to Providence, Rhode Island, where I was a freshman in college. When they arrived, I couldn't figure out what they were doing there in person. In my self-absorbed collegiate state, I thought maybe they were worried about my brewing insomnia. I took them to the women's center to show them where I'd been volunteering. Then they sat me down in the cozy common room and my mother shut the door, saying they'd come because they had to tell me something. I was bewildered. It was too hard for my father to say the words. My mother told me the bad news while my father looked away and held my hand. By the time he was diagnosed, the cancer was everywhere, in the back, in the bones, the organs.

Most people think Kafka is surreal. I don't. Anyone who has had a strange illness knows that Kafka is a master of realism. One day you wake up and you are a bug. One day you wake up and your face is crooked. One day my father woke up and he could not walk and it turned out cancer was riddling his whole body. When I first read *The Metamorphosis*, I wept for Gregor Samsa.

During that strange weekend visit to Providence, my parents took me and some of my friends out to a Chinese restaurant. There was laughter, there was food. At the end of the meal, there were fortune cookies. We all cracked ours open.

My father's fortune was blank.

We all looked away and changed the subject.

Carl Jung once said that your three earliest memories form the leitmotif of your life. My earliest memories are: jumping into a swimming pool in Iowa before I knew how to swim, being submerged, and my father rescuing me. Being knocked down by a wave in the Atlantic Ocean and having my father haul me back up again. And being at a hotel lobby, twirling, mad with joy, dizzy, looking up for my father, hugging him around the legs, and then screaming—it was a stranger I had mistaken for my father. Is this my theme? My father rescuing me when I was submerged, then the search for my father and finding him missing? That seems far too tidy for a leitmotif.

Me and my father at my aunt's wedding.

My father would joke when he was sick. The experimental radiation he was undergoing made his urine toxic, so he joked about how he would outlive us all and piss on our graves with toxic pee. He wanted to live long enough to go one last time as a family to Cape Cod, where we had often gone in the summer. He was too sick to go that last summer. We pretended to have Cape Cod from home. We ate fish and wrote postcards from his yellow sickroom.

Shortly afterward he had a blood clot, and his white blood cell count became dangerously low, so he went into the hospital for the last time. The whole extended family gathered to say good-bye. My grandmother, my mother's mother, was sideswiped to see him in that hospital bed, how changed he was—she bent over and bellowed. My father had said he was grateful that his parents were already dead, so they would not see him go first.

I read to him in the hospital from his favorite poets—Dylan Thomas and E. E. Cummings. His favorite poem was "Fern Hill." "Now as I was young and easy under the apple boughs / About the lilting house and happy as the grass was green. . . ." That was my father's childhood in Iowa, I thought. "I was prince of the apple towns . . . And wake to the farm forever fled from the childless land. . . ." My father's people were not farmers . . . but they lived among farms.

My father even had a lampshade given to him by the caretaker at Dylan Thomas's house. He and my mother had gone on a pilgrimage to Wales during their honeymoon to see the house where Dylan Thomas had just died. Thomas's caretaker was giving away mementos to pilgrims. "Take a lampshade. And some rosemary for remembrance from the garden." Later I found this green lampshade, which looked like a Victorian doll skirt, crushed in my closet and I hung it up in my room.

"Time held me green and dying / Though I sang in my chains like the sea."

My father used to put on jazz records for me to listen to in the room we called the cold room. The room was called the cold room because it was cold; the windows must have leaked in air. But it was warm because it was where we played and put on records and where my sister and I invented dance routines.

My father would explain to me how Dave Brubeck's "Take Five" was written in a 5/4 time signature, difficult to achieve. He revered Dave Brubeck. He also revered the Dave Brubeck Quartet's saxophonist, Paul Desmond, who died of lung cancer at the age of fifty-two. By a twist of fate, my father once found himself sitting next to Dave Brubeck on one of those rent-a-car shuttles leaving an airport. My father recognized Dave, told him he was a childhood hero, and they got to talking. Dave Brubeck told my father how Paul Desmond would perform while sick; that while essentially dying, he would blow the last note on his saxophone with all of his might, then the curtain would come down, and he would collapse, and the band would carry him offstage.

When my father was dying (at the same age), he was his own

version of Paul Desmond. My father's version of playing a saxophone with all his might was to be entirely present with the people around him. He put them at ease, told jokes, asked how they were doing, remembered the details of their daily lives. He was also blowing his saxophone when he was first diagnosed with cancer, and having just been out of work for a year, he kept driving to his new job in Racine, Wisconsin, from Chicago every day—an hour and a half drive—sometimes buying his family a Wisconsin pastry delicacy called kringle on the way home. He had to keep his job to keep his health insurance once he was sick. He had to support his family. And he had to keep his mind occupied, driving on a long boring interstate, that was another way of blowing his horn. And he blew his horn when he insisted on normalcy, insisted I keep going to college, rather than taking a leave of absence to, as he put it, spend my youth emptying his bedpan.

Instead, he would write me long letters, which maybe he composed in his head on those long drives to Racine, about the nature of unconditional love and the origins of poetry. I came home from college at every opportunity. One day, at home on a break, I saw him walking to the bathroom quickly, and his pants fell down around his ankles. He had lost so much weight, and he couldn't pull his pants up himself. I knew that this was one of the many things he did not want me to see—one of the many reasons he wanted me back at college, pretending a degree of normalcy I did not feel.

And at the end, in a grim hospital, he made people laugh—that was how he blew his saxophone.

His oncologist, an Orthodox Jewish man, visited my father in the hospital and told him that he had tumors all over the lung. He said with philosophical gentleness that it could be days, or it could be months. Somehow his religious, philosophical nature comforted my father more than the secular doctors. My father told us he wanted a full band to play "When the Saints Go Marching In" at his funeral.

During those last few days in the hospital, my father told my mother that she was his tether. Then he couldn't speak, but he could listen. My mother told him that it was all right for him to go. He was untethered.

I was driving then, lost in some godforsaken northwest suburb of Chicago near the hospital, looking for God knows what, sent on some kind of errand. When I came back, the whole family was assembled. The moon outside was rising. Come quickly, they said. My father was grasping at the bedsheets, looking up. Then his breath entered the room, a warmth entered my body, and he was gone.

My mother hugged his body—there was almost nothing left of him—and then she moaned, "Oh, oh, I cracked his ribs. I hurt him. . . ." My uncle told her gently that nothing could hurt him anymore.

At least that is what I remember. Memory is not to be trusted entirely after a death. I think of my father's death like a blurry hole in the pages of a childhood book. In *The Very Hungry Caterpillar*, the caterpillar eats a little hole out of one page, and every page you turn has a little hole in it. I do know that the band at the Congregational Church in Wilmette, Illinois, did play "When the Saints Go Marching In."

There is a Buddhist parable called "The Farmer's Luck," otherwise known as "Maybe." The tale follows a young man who breaks his leg while horseback riding and all the neighbors say, "What bad luck!"

And his parents say, "Maybe."

The next day, the army comes by to draft all the young men in the village, but the broken-legged man is spared from going to war because of his leg. The neighbors all say, "What good luck!"

And the parents say, "Maybe."

And I think back to the fortune cookie I got after I learned I was pregnant with twins: "Deliver what is inside you, and it will save your life."

On the most basic medical level, delivering my twins caused a non-life-threatening paralysis of my face; but that paralysis ended up revealing a potentially lifesaving diagnosis that affected my whole family.

Maybe my babies saved my life and the life of their older sister, Anna, quite literally. In that sense, maybe Bell's palsy was a tremendous gift.

And so I've grown to love the syllables in the word *maybe*. Today my head is full of maybes. Maybe healing is not linear. Maybe there is no one health care savior but many patient practitioners. Maybe the long haul is longer than anticipated. Maybe a nap is in order. Maybe writing down your story helps. Maybe, outside your immediate field of vision, someone down the block is learning how to stand on one leg again; someone is learning to smile again; someone is learning to breathe again; and someone is relearning their place on this earth with a new asymmetry they could never have foretold and you *can only imagine.* Single breast, single leg, single lung, single kidney, single hand.

And maybe these asymmetries are not equal in terms of how suffering is doled out. And maybe false equivalencies are just as bad as deciding not to even try to imagine another person's pain. And maybe we are all seeking a cure of some kind.

CHAPTER 32

A Woman Slowly Gets Better

The Roman god Janus has two faces, one looking backwards and one looking forwards. The fact that humans have only one face, on one side of our bodies, is perhaps a sign of our perceptual limitations. (As that wonderful actor told me long ago, "Unfortunately my penis is on the same side of my body as my face.") We are not owls. Nor can we see the world in 360 degrees. Our faces are how we see and how we are seen. But the gods have more faces to look with. Should we aspire to have extra invisible faces with which to see reality? Or just pray to the gods who know more, who see more, than we can?

Janus's face has a gateway to the past and to the future. I start to think of my face this way, as having a gate to the past and the future, rather than being fixed in time.

After all that physical therapy, it's not that I'm suddenly perfectly symmetrical, or that all of my synkinesis magically went away, or that my smile looks the way it did when I was thirty. I still hate being photographed, and Hope still looks at pictures of me at my wedding and says matter-of-factly, "You were so much prettier then."

On the other hand, my Alexander Technique teacher, on a Zoom call, suddenly couldn't tell, at rest, which side of my face had the palsy. And at my last Zoom physical therapy meeting, Elaine told me to go out and buy a bottle of wine—she gave me an 82 percent score on muscle movement. That is progress.

Recently, my daughter Hope took this picture of me. She caught a moment. I am stretching towards something . . . what? A slow movement towards joy?

I am still half-hidden from you in that photograph. It is not a full Allen Ginsberg. Something is still partial, unrevealed. I still recoil from giving you a forced, photographable joy. The joy comes unbidden. The joy comes, as the poet Audre Lorde says about profoundly embodied joy, "from within outward," rather than from outside in, a calculated response to the camera's silent appraisal.

A former student, a wonderful playwright named Tori Sampson, wrote a play called *If Pretty Hurts Ugly Must Be a Muhfucka.* It's an adaptation of a West African fable about jealous girls who try to drown the most beautiful girl in the village. At the end of the play, a woman sits at the mirror and slowly puts on makeup. She says to herself in the mirror, like a mantra: "This is my body. I am my soul. These are my lips. I am my word. This is my skin. I am my action. These are my legs. I am my contribution. This is my smile. I am my laughter."

This is my smile. I am my laughter.

Tonight my husband says to me in the dark of our bed, "Turn on the lights. I want to see your face."

There is a mirror next to the very slow elevator in my building. Sometimes I do my facial exercises there while waiting. This morning my kids are in tow, waiting for me to walk them to school. I smile in the mirror. I purse my lips. They watch me.

Then they say, unbidden, "Don't do that, Mama; we like your half smile; your face looks weird with a big smile."

I realize suddenly, after all my fears about not being able to smile at my babies, they accept my face. In fact, they have always accepted my face. And not only have they accepted my face; they have divined my intentions. They have understood that my half smile was always intended, for them, as, quite simply, a smile.

And now it seems so obvious—the children loved me and knew that they were loved *by* me not for or from my features but for something else, something well below the surface of my fascia.

And I think of Alice Walker's dedication of her book to her daughter: "Who saw in me / what I considered / a scar / And re-defined it / as / a world." Walker's daughter had for the first time noticed that one of her mother's eyes was scarred, from a child-hood accident. Instead of saying something cruel, her daughter said, "There's a world in your eye."

I begin to think not: What is your mirror? But: *Who* is your mirror?

* * *

In the Ingmar Bergman film *Fanny and Alexander*, Gustav says, "My dear, dear friends. . . . My wisdom is simple. . . . We must live in the little world. Don't be sad, dear splendid artists. Actors and actresses, we need you all the same. . . . The world is a den of thieves and night is falling. . . . Let us be kind, generous, affectionate, and good. It is necessary and not at all shameful, to take pleasure in the little world."

To take pleasure in the little world.

For me, the little world is both the theater and my home, with all of its attendant children.

In the Bergman film, there is no conflict implied between the two little worlds. Unlike in Ibsen's *A Doll's House*, where Nora must slam the door and walk out of the dollhouse in order to attain political liberation, Gustav is calling for both men and women to attend to the small things in order to attain the big things, in order to attain spiritual liberation.

And at this moment, this feels right to me—the call to take pleasure in the little worlds, both of the little worlds that I have been so lucky to inhabit.

My best friend from childhood, Sarah, is a pediatrician, and she is both practical and kind. We were talking about my face one day. "It's not a tragedy," she said, "but it must be disappointing." I suppose this helpful distinction between the disappointing and the tragic sheds light on why I resisted writing about Bell's palsy for such a long time. Disappointing things were not for the written word, disappointing things were for the stiff upper lip. Tragic things are for the written word, because in tragedy there is catharsis, not slow, incremental, almost invisible progress.

The partial recovery is not terribly dramatic. It is the stuff of life, not art. But the partial recovery is, I believe, very much like life. Most people have partially recovered from something. A childhood burn, a childhood trauma, a broken bone, a broken heart. . . . How rare is it for someone to hear proclaimed about their heart or their body: "You have made a full recovery." Who, after all, is fully recovered from life? Our bodies are resilient but always in the process of dying, even as they sometimes have the grace to regenerate.

I can now endure the self-consciousness of endless Zoom calls, watching myself talk. And I realize that almost all sane people hate looking at their own faces on Zoom, Bell's palsy or no Bell's palsy. I no longer fear that strangers cannot interpret my affect. I can laugh without extreme self-consciousness. I have relearned how to smile for pictures. And that phrase haunts me for what it is: "Smile for the camera." Not smile for yourself, not smile for your own joy—but smile for an inanimate object. I can do it if I have to. But it is no more the measure of my joy than a table-spoon could be the measure of my heart.

Without my crooked smile, I might never have parsed the dif-ference between disappointment and tragedy for that length of time. I would have never known, in such an intimate way, that people are smiling behind their masks. I would not have had that particular lesson of endurance, when your body does not obey your heart.

I would also never have learned how adaptable the body and mind are, how one function takes over another lost function. I may not have been smiling in photos with my babies when they were small, but when I watch old videos, I realize that I was com-

municating joy and love with my *voice* constantly when I was behind the camera. The voice was smiling, when the face was not.
And if you find your voice, you might refuse the image.

I listened for way too long to the wrong story about my face.
I listened to a neurological expert who said that after six months
my nerves would no longer grow, and that it didn't matter if I did
anything to help my face. He turned out to be wrong on both
counts. It's not uncommon for women to listen to and believe the
wrong stories about their own faces. Not only was I listening to
the wrong narrative, I was writing the wrong narrative about my
illness inside my own mind, a narrative full of shame and blame.
It took me ten years not only to find the right experts but to trust
myself as the expert of my own story.

Youngey Mingyur Rinpoche, a Tibetan monk who once left
the comfort of his robes and monastery to travel with absolutely
nothing—no money, no lodging, no food—writes of how we all
have to contend with birth, aging, sickness, and death, but that
"they can be experienced without extras, without compounding
the suffering with story lines that solidify our misperceptions."

As a writer I should have been aware that the shape of a story
can make things worse.

It took me a decade to change my narrative about my face. Or
to leave the story alone. To let the muscles be merely the muscles
on my face, and to use my ability to make up stories in the service
of making up other, different stories.

I woke up from a dream this morning in which I was saying, "In
a nutshell, I am not a nutshell."

The ends of stories are places to put nutshells, lessons. This
is my big chance to tell you how I walked a Pilgrim's Progress,
out of the slough of despond into the Celestial City (Brooklyn?).

I am suspicious of lessons, and morals that I might extract from suffering, so why do I continue to seek them?

I am with the children at a bay in Cape Cod, visiting Paula, the same teacher who told me I'd write again after having three children, the same teacher who said she'd take care of me and then did. Now, again, she is making a place for me to write, given me a desk, and all the Yorkshire tea I want to drink.

The twins are looking for shells on the beach. They arrange them on the sand. "Which is your favorite?" they ask me. I choose a small, iridescent broken shell. "But don't you like this one?" they ask, pointing to a less broken, more perfect, bland shell.

"No, I like the broken shell," I say. "It's iridescent."

And I think: imperfection is a portal. Whereas perfection and symmetry create distance. Our culture values perfect pictures of ourselves, mirage, over and above authentic connection. But we meet one another through the imperfect particular of our bodies. Imperfection calls out for affinity—for the beloved to say, I too am broken, but may I join you?

What if I stopped thinking of the smile as a flash of symmetry but instead as a flash of affinity? An imperfect admission of the simple desire to connect? It is perhaps in our asymmetry that we come to belong to one another. Fragility invites care.

Symmetry is complete unto itself. Asymmetry calls out to a beloved to complete it.

Japanese poetry, which celebrates the hidden, the implied, and impermanence, is asymmetrical. The haiku has an uneven number of syllables (five, seven, five) and the three lines call out to the reader to supply the invisible fourth line with an answering thought. Japanese aesthetics also celebrates *wabi-sabi*—the idea that imperfection is a doorway into a piece of art. And so

I've been practicing writing haiku, thinking about the flaw in the weave. In Navajo weaving, rugs often have a spirit line—an apparent asymmetry—that allows the spirit of the weaver to exit the rug. In Islamic architecture, asymmetries are purposefully built into buildings, to reflect the notion that God can be perfect and we are not.

This haiku took me, in a sense, ten years to write:

A crooked smile is
better than a crooked heart;
open me to God

My years of writing plays tells me that a story requires an apotheosis, a sudden transformation. But my story has been so slow, so incremental; the chronic resists plot and epiphany. When diseases and stories are chronic, doctors and writers often both run for the hills.

A woman slowly gets better.

What kind of story is that?

I know that in the writing of the story itself, *A woman slowly gets better*, I slowly did get better. Not completely better. I will probably always have a crooked smile. But I am better enough. Better enough for strangers to know if I am trying to be friendly. Better enough for my intimates to know if I am full of joy. Better enough to *proceed*. To paint the self-portrait now, not later, not to wait to be fully healed to go on with life. To proceed, to move— slowly or quickly or at any pace at all—but to defy stasis.

For some reason what I had always seemed to know about art—that perfection was not the goal; that the appearance of perfect craft was static and sealed the heart, whereas imperfection and the messy particular had the power to open the heart—I forgot to apply to parenting or to my own face. This concept of the good enough face I was ready now to join with the concept of the good enough mother. I was good enough to proceed with the fundamental purpose in life: to give and to receive love.

The more Buddhist I get, the more Catholic I get. I can't help it. It's like going forth in the snow, pulling one's childhood sled behind.

As I near the end of this story, what I would like to say to myself is this: I would like to accept my face, my story, as it is written on my face, my joy.

And what I would like to tell you, reader, though I don't know you, though I have never met you, is: I love your face.

I love your eyes reading across the page—the wrinkles, the furrowed brow, whatever asymmetries you might have, whether it's a yellow snaggletooth like mine or a crooked smile like mine—all the lines denoting story. This mole, that scar, all our protuberances, battle-scarred, wounded, incomplete; almost healed, barely healed, or never going to be healed in the outward sense, not in this lifetime—scar tissued or just plain growing older—oh, how beautiful you are. I want to cherish the wrinkle that is a marker of whatever it is that makes your joy hard-won and human.

A little prayer:

May all the broken faces heal.
May what appears to be broken, actually be in the midst
    of an untold, unforeseeable healing.

Acknowledgments

Writing plays, one mostly lets time unfold in the present tense. Putting a chronic illness in the past tense felt like a victory over time and space, a catharsis in and of itself; and I would never have been able to wrap my head around the vagaries of tense without the incisive, compassionate, always present editor Marysue Rucci. Her way into the material was always as insightful as it was personal and give me permission, literally and metaphorically, to put the healing in the present tense. I am ever grateful for the extraordinary Dorian Karchmar's impeccable eye and ear and judgment as a literary agent. And for Emma Feiwel's reading of multiple drafts and never-flagging encouragement and advice. I would also like to thank Albert Lee, who listened to me with great care when I was at the early stages of dreaming up this book and who told me there was a book here. And Katie Adams also gave wonderful, supportive advice as I dove into the first pages of the manuscript.

In most of this book, my life in the theater is offstage and in the background, but there are some beloved theater collaborators I've worked with again and again and I must thank them for their lifelong sustenance: David Adjmi, Todd Almond, Alexandra Beller, André Bishop, Anne Bogart, Anne Cattaneo, Melissa Crespo, Todd London, Emily Mann, Lisa McNulty, Emily Morse, Bruce Ostler, Mark Subias, Rebecca Taichman,

Les Waters, Mark Wing-Davey, and Anita Yavich. And I want to thank James Bundy, who is in large part responsible for how I began to be produced in the American theater and who made possible my joy in teaching, and also happens to be responsible for guiding me towards Alexander Technique for Bell's palsy. Thank you to John Lahr for the conversations. And to my extended theater family who has read these pages in early forms: Beth Henley, Joyce Piven, Jessica Thebus, Polly Noonan, and P. Carl. I have so much tenderness and gratitude for each of you.

My pickle council is a group of writers I share pages and pickles with. The pickles can be real or metaphorical, and my council has all read versions of this manuscript, and I am so grateful for them: Kathleen Tolan, Andy Bragen, Lily Thorne, Keith Reddin, and Jorge Ignacio Cortiñas. Kathleen and Andy also appear in many places in this book, and I thank them for all of those appearances in life and art. It's a lonely business being a playwright unless you decide at the outset that playwrights make the best kinds of friends. Julia Cho is one such friend. She and Karen Zacarias, Kathleen Tolan, Julia Jordan, Lynn Nottage, Quiara Alegería Hudes, and Amy Herzog show me what grace looks like on a mother who writes.

I was so lucky to meet the wonderful writer and thinker James Shapiro in the last few years, to have lucked into regular literary lunches with him and the great poet Paul Muldoon. James gave me so much encouragement about this book—looked me in the eye and helped me dream it into being and then, for good measure, read multiple drafts. He and his wife, the wonderful writer and teacher Mary Cregan, both gave me indispensable feedback and moral support and I couldn't be more grateful.

I am indebted to so many actors who are my heroes and my avatars and my community. I want to thank a few in particular here who appear in the pages of this book. Thank you to Rachel

Weisz for reading and for your friendship. Thank you to Crystal Finn for reading drafts and telling me about Matisse and the Jungian dictionary of symbols. Thank you to Jessica Hecht for providing me refuge in your home when I worked on the first draft during the summer. Thank you to the amazing Laura Benanti and Michael Cerveris, who appear in these pages and whom I would walk over fire for, just to hear my words in their mouths. And from that same cast—dear Quincy Tyler Bernstine, Maria Dizzia, Wendy Rich Stetson, and Thomas Jay Ryan. Thank you to Frances McDormand for telling me about physical therapy and for not giving a rat's ass about how women are supposed to age in this deformed culture—for saying with your words and actions that the culture of plastic surgery is deformed, aging women are not. Thank you to Mary-Louise Parker for dropping that card off at my apartment on my birthday—you knew just the right words. To Kathleen Chalfant for your eternal friendship and example, and to the whole *Peter Pan* extended family. To Jonathan Kalb, theater critic and fellow traveler, who gave me a magical mirror that is called compassion.

For my teachers in the Buddhist tradition, Khenpo Pema Wangdak, who told me I could smile on a train; William Duprey, who has taught me meditation for twenty years and counting; Mark Epstein, who saves lives on a daily basis; and Tenzin Palmo, with whom I took refuge. Thanks to my little dharma group, Emily and Stephen. And thank you to Yangzom, who began as our babysitter and who is in so many ways my teacher. It makes sense that I would entrust the care of my children to someone whom I would also trust with the care of my spirit.

To old friends who have given me so much joy, and some of whom have read drafts: Sarah Hinkel Sullivan, Erin Crowley, Sarah Fulford, Sherry Mason, Mindy Sobota, Luke Walden, Sarah Geraghty, Nicole Rose, Katie Lussier, Jacob Appel, Sarah Curtis, JoJo Karlin, Mari and Rick Tetzeli, Nicholas Dawidoff, James

Platt, Jill Dawsey, Kirsten Deluca, Jeremy Giller. I'm so grateful for your friendship. Special thanks to Robyn Tamura for helping me get through this pandemic.

To my students, whom I adore beyond measure, one of whom—Miranda Rose Hall—read a draft of this book early on and also gave me some very good advice, and then continued to be in dialogue with me as I finished it. Thank you to Tori Sampson for her incredible *If Pretty Hurts*. To Amelia Roper, Rachel Kauder Nalebuff. And to Max Ritvo: I wish I could share this book with you. And all of you present and former students who inspire me on a daily basis.

To the incredible Western doctors who helped me through this time—to Dr. Russell Chin for his extraordinary diagnostic powers, to heroic Dr. Michael Silverstein, who delivered Hope and William safely. To Dr. Christina Tennyson and Dr. Julie Foont, the most angelic gastroenterologists. To Dr. Julie Roth, a long-time friend and neurologist who so patiently answered all of my questions and gave me hope and insight. And to Dr. Chu for her gentleness and care. And thank you to Dr. Claudia Cooke and Dr. Alfred Miller.

To the Eastern doctors, the healers, the outside-the-box doctors, who helped me so much when I'd exhausted the resources of Western medicine: Elaine Borja-Jaffe, Rebecca Krauss, Elaine Stern, Charles Nicolai, Jessica Wolf, Isis Medina, Zoe Kogan. Zoe—there aren't many (or any other?) acupuncturists who make you laugh your ass off while lying on a table with needles in your face, who can also offer the best literary advice and give you the best herbs, standing on a corner, during a pandemic.

To my teachers: Paula Vogel and Anne Fausto Sterling. What can I put on a page that expresses what you've given our family? It started with playwriting and the classroom but became about life itself. How to pick a cucumber. How to model generosity for the next generation. How to love your partner over time. I'm sitting in the periwinkle room that you've loaned me while I write these acknowledgments. You've fed me literal food and figurative food ever since I met you. How will I ever feed you back?

To Tina Howe, who gave me a pink Ganesh at my first preview in New York, and told me that 9 a.m. to 3 p.m. are the perfect hours to write in anyway, and so it was perfectly possible to be a mother and a writer. To the playwright Chuck Mee, who wrote so beautifully in *A Nearly Normal Life*, "Illness damages our aesthetic sense of our lives—and that is a source of suffering. . . . The aesthetic whole of a life must be reconstructed if a person is to regain a sense of coherence."

Thank you for that lesson, and for giving my play *Eurydice* to Les Waters when I was twenty-seven. To all my colleagues at Yale who teach me so much and who have always been wonderfully supportive of balancing motherhood with teaching, including Tarell McCraney, Anne Erbe, Jennifer Kiger, and Jackie Sibblies Drury.

To the ancestors, to all the Kehoes, to Elizabeth Charuvastra and all my understanding in-laws, Marcus and Nicole. To my father, Patrick Ruhl. A long time ago you wrote me a letter when you were sick. And you told me everything I needed to go on in life without you.

There are really no words to thank my mother, Kathleen Ruhl, for bringing me into this world, teaching me to love theater, teaching me to love, period. To my sister, Kate, for staying up all night with me feeding the twins during that insane time, for being my rock, for laughing me out of myself.

To my dear ones, my children! Anna! William! Hope! You get exclamation points. I love you to the moon and back. I hope you don't mind when you grow up that I nattered on about my postpartum condition here. Every moment of being in the world with you joyful three is a gift. The gift of asymmetry—the gift of three.

Anna read part of this book recently and said: "I always thought of your face as a beautiful house. A wall suddenly fell down, and you tried to rebuild it, brick by brick. And you couldn't quite. And all you saw was the wall. But all we saw was our house." Thank you, dear Anna.

And to Tony—Tony, Tony, Tony—how can I thank you? A haiku I wrote for you recently . . .

Love poem to my husband who fixed the
Scotch tape dispenser today

The tape was unseen,
trapped in itself; you found the
beginning again.

Resources and Sources

RESOURCES

There are many resources for the below challenges; I just wanted to share a few ideas for those who might need a place to start.

If you or a loved one has cholestasis of the liver during pregnancy:

Intrahepatic Cholestasis of Pregnancy (https://icpcare.org)

If you or a loved one has celiac disease:

Celiac Disease Center at Columbia University (www.celiacdiseasecenter
    .columbia.edu)
Gluten Is My Bitch: Rants, Recipes, and Ridiculousness for the Gluten-Free by
    April Peveteaux (New York: Stewart, Tabori & Chang, 2015); also
    her blog, *Gluten is my Bitch*
Gluten-Free Girl and the Chef: A Love Story with 100 Tempting Recipes, by
    Shauna James Ahern and Daniel Ahern (Hoboken, NJ: Wiley, 2010)

If you or a loved one has postpartum depression:

Seleni (www.seleni.org)
Pospartum Support International (www.psidirectory.com)
This Isn't What I Expected: Overcoming Postpartum Depression, 2nd edition, by
    Karen R. Kleiman and Valerie Davis Raskin (New York: Hachette, 2013)

If you or a loved one has unremitting Bell's palsy:

Center for Facial Recovery, Baltimore, Maryland
        (https://facialrecovery.com/)
Facial Palsy UK (facialpalsy.org.uk)
Facial Paralysis & Reanimation Center, NYU Langone Health, New York
        (https://nyulangone.org/locations/facial-paralysis-reanimation-center)
Facial Paralysis Institute, Los Angeles
        (https://www.facialparalysisinstitute.com/)

Keep looking for the right specialist until you find someone
you connect with who can help you, whether it's a neurologist,
physical therapist, acupuncturist, chiropractor, or internal medicine doctor who can prescribe antivirals and steroids at the right
moment and test you for Lyme disease, specifically, Borreliosis,
which can be difficult to detect.

This book is not the end of my story, nor of yours. Don't give up.

SOURCES IN ORDER OF APPEARANCE

Literary and Theatrical Works

Alice Walker, *In Search of Our Mother's Gardens* (1983; reprint, Boston:
        Mariner Books, 2003). First quote: "Someone asked me once
        whether I thought women artists should have children, and, since
        we were beyond discussing why this question is never asked artists
        who are men, I gave my answer promptly. 'Yes,' I said, somewhat
        to my surprise. And, as if to amend my rashness, I added: 'They
        should have children—assuming this is of interest to them—but only
        one.' . . . Because with one child you can move. With more than one
        you're a sitting duck." Second quote: "Since her birth I have worried
        about her discovery that her mother's eyes are different from other
        people's. Will she be embarrassed? I think. What will she say? Every
        day she watches a television program called *Big Blue Marble*. It begins

with a picture of the Earth as it appears from the moon. It is bluish, a little battered-looking, but full of light. . . . One day when I am putting Rebecca down for her nap, she suddenly focuses on my eye. Something inside me cringes, gets ready to try to protect myself. All children are cruel about physical differences. . . . But no-o-o-o . . . She even holds my face maternally between her dimpled little hands . . . 'Mommy, there's a world in your eye. . . . Mommy, where did you get that world in your eye?'"

Charlotte Perkins Gilman, "The Yellow Wall Paper," *New England Magazine*, January 1892. "Sometimes I think there are a great many women behind, and sometimes only one, and she crawls around fast, and her crawling shakes it all over. . . . And she is all the time trying to climb through. But nobody could climb through that pattern—it strangles so."

Virginia Woolf, *Mrs. Dalloway* (New York: Harcourt, 1925).

Antoine de Saint-Exupéry, *The Little Prince*, trans. Katherine Woods (New York: Reynal & Hitchcock, 1943).

Elizabeth Bishop, "The Art of Poetry No. 27," interview by Elizabeth Spires, *Paris Review*, no. 80 (Summer 1981), https://www .theparisreview.org/interviews/3229/the-art-of-poetry-no-27 -elizabeth-bishop.

Daaimah Mubashshir, *The Immeasurable Want of Light* (Brooklyn, NY: 3Hole-Press, 2018).

Eugène Ionesco, *The Bald Soprano*, trans. Donald M. Allen (New York: Grove Press, 1958).

Charlotte Brontë, *Villette* (1853; reprint, London: Penguin Books, 1985).

Susan Sontag, *Illness as Metaphor* (New York: Farrar, Straus and Giroux, 1978).

William Blake, "The Tyger" (1794).

Ken Campbell, *Pigspurt: Or Six Pigs from Happiness* (London: Methuen Drama, 1993).

Charles L. Mee, *A Nearly Normal Life* (New York: Little, Brown, 2000).

Audre Lorde, "The Uses of Anger: Women Responding to Racism," in *Sister Outsider: Essays and Speeches* (Berkeley, CA: Crossing Press, 1984).

Flannery O'Connor, *A Prayer Journal* (New York: Farrar, Straus and Giroux, 2013).

Simone Weil, *First and Last Notebooks: Supernatural Knowledge*, trans. Roger Rees (1970; reprint, Eugene, OR: Wipf & Stock, 2015).

Ludwig Bemelmans, *Madeline* (1939; reprint, New York: Puffin Books, 1998).

Milan Kundera, *The Unbearable Lightness of Being* (1984; reprint, New York: Harper Perennial Modern Classics, 1999).

William Shakespeare, *The Winter's Tale* (1611).

William Butler Yeats, "When You Are Old," in *The Rose* (1893).

Amanda Berenguer, "A Study in Wrinkles," in *Materia Prima*, ed. Kristin Dykstra and Kent Johnson, trans. Gillian Brassil, Anna Deeny Morales, Mónica de la Torre, Urayoán Noel, Jeannine Marie Pitas, and Alex Verdolin (Brooklyn, NY: Ugly Duckling Press, 2019).

Dylan Thomas, "Fern Hill" (1945).

Tori Sampson, *If Pretty Hurts Ugly Must Be a Muhfucka* (New York: Samuel French, 2020).

Spiritual, Psychological, and Philosophical Works

Thich Nhat Hanh, *Anger: Wisdom for Cooling the Flames* (New York: Riverhead Books, 2001).

Thich Nhat Hanh, *Peace Is Every Step: The Path of Mindfulness in Everyday Life* (1991; reprint, New York: Bantam Books, 1992): "Even if we spend a lot of money on gifts for everyone in our family, nothing we buy could give them as much happiness as the gift of our awareness, our smile. And this precious gift costs nothing."

Heraclitus, *The Fragments of Heraclitus*, trans. G. T. W. Patrick.

Donald W. Winnicott, *Playing and Reality* (1971; reprint, Oxford: Routledge, 2005).

Serene Jones, *Call It Grace: Finding Meaning in a Fractured World* (2019; reprint, New York: Penguin, 2020).

Shantideva, *The Way of the Bodhisattva: A Translation of the Bodhicharyavatara* (Boston: Shambhala Publications, 1997).

Koun Yamada, trans., *The Gateless Gate: The Classic Book of Zen Koans* (Somerville, MA: Wisdom, 2004).

Youngey Mingyur Rinpoche with Helen Tworkov, *In Love with the World: A Monk's Journey Through the Bardos of Living and Dying* (New York: Spiegel & Grau, 2019).

Playlist

"Make 'Em Laugh," by Betty Comden and Adolph Green, sung by Donald O'Connor, from *Singin' in the Rain* (1952).

"I've Grown Accustomed to Her Face," lyrics by Alan Jay Lerner, music by Frederick Loewe, from *My Fair Lady* (1956).

"Smile," lyrics by John Turner and Geoffrey Parsons, music by Charlie Chaplin, sung by Nat King Cole (1954).

Fanny and Alexander, written and directed by Ingmar Bergman (1982).

Paintings, Mentioned and Included

Tatyana Fazlalizadeh, *Stop Telling Women to Smile* (2012).

Leonardo da Vinci (1452–1519). *Mona Lisa (La Gioconda)*. Oil on wood, 77 x 53 cm. INV779. Photo: Michel Urtado 2011. © RMN-Grand Palais / Art Resource, NY.

Johannes Vermeer, *Woman in Blue Reading a Letter* (c. 1663). Rijksmuseum, Amsterdam.

Henri Matisse, *Plum Blossoms, Green Background* (1948).

Gustave Moreau (1826–1898). *Helen on the Ramparts of Troy*. Oil on canvas. 100 x 61 cm. Inv. No. Cat. 58. Photo: René-Gabriel Ojeda © RMN-Grand Palais / Art Resource, NY

Photographs

Opening night of *In the Next Room*: Bruce Glikas/FilmMagic

Vanity Fair: Tina Tyrell

Sarah in coat and scarf at an opening: Jamie McCarthy/Getty Images

Allen Ginsberg: Michiel Hendryckx

Wedding photographs courtesy of my friend Kathleen Hinkel; all other photographs courtesy of the author

Medical and Scientific Works

Lisa Lerer, "Bedrest Is Bunk, *Atlantic*, August 2018, https://www.theatlantic.com/family/archive/2018/08/bed-rest-is-bunk/566858/.

Christina A. McCall, David A. Grimes, and Anne Drapkin Lyerly, " 'Therapeutic' Bed Rest in Pregnancy: Unethical and Unsupported by Data," *Journal of Obstetrics and Gynecology* 121, no. 6 (June 2013): 1305–8; https://doi.org/10.1097/AOG.0b013e318293f12f.

Rachel Maines, *The Technology of Orgasm: "Hysteria," the Vibrator, and Women's Sexual Satisfaction* (Baltimore: Johns Hopkins University Press, 1999).

Abbey Perreault, "The 'Father of American Neurology' Prescribed Women Months of Motionless Milk Drinking," *Atlas Obscura*, September 28, 2018, https://www.atlasobscura.com/articles/what-was-the-rest-cure.

Marian F. MacDorman, Eugene Declerq, Howard Cabral, and Christine Morton, "Recent Increases in the U.S. Maternal Mortality Rate: Disentangling Trends from Measurement Issues," *Obstetrics and Gynecology* 128, no. 3 (September 2016): 447–55, https://doi.org/10.1097/AOG.0000000000001556.

Roni Caryn Rabin, "Huge Racial Disparities Found in Deaths Linked to Pregnancy," *New York Times*, May 7, 2019, https://www.nytimes.com/2019/05/07/health/pregnancy-deaths-.html.

Mohammad M. Sajadi, Mohamad-Reza M. Sajadi, and Seyed Mahmoud Tabatabaie, "The History of Facial Palsy and Spasm: Hippocrates to Razi," *Neurology* 77, no. 2 (July 2011): 174–78, https://doi.org/10.1212/WNL.0b013e3182242d23.

Alina Lukashevsky, "The Science of Genuine Smiles," *HuffPost*, March 28, 2016, https://www.huffpost.com/entry/the-science-behind-smiles_b_9448650.

Guillaume Duchenne, *The Mechanism of Human Facial Expression*, 1862; edited and translated by R. Andrew Cuthbertson (Cambridge: Cambridge University Press, 1990).

Walter Isaacson, "The Science Behind Mona Lisa's Smile," *Atlantic*, November 2017, https://www.theatlantic.com/magazine/archive/2017/11/leonardo-da-vinci-mona-lisa-smile/540636/.

Alessandro Soranzo and Michelle Newberry, "The Uncatchable Smile in Leonardo da Vinci's La Bella Principessa Portrait," *Vision Research* 113, Part A (August 2015): 78–86, https://doi.org/10.1016/j.visres.2015.05.014.

Luca Marsili, Lucia Ricciardi, and Matteo Bologna, "Unraveling the Asymmetry of Mona Lisa Smile," *Cortex* 120 (November 2019): 607–10, https://doi.org/10.1016/j.cortex.2019.03.020.

Charles Darwin, *The Expression of the Emotions in Man and Animals* (New York: D. Appleton, 1872), 65.

Steven Brown, Peter Cockett, and Ye Yuan, "The Neuroscience of *Romeo and Juliet*: An fMRI Study of Acting," *Royal Society of Open Science* 6, no. 3 (March 2019), https://doi.org/10.1098/rsos.181908.

Kelsey Blackburn and James Schrillio, "Emotive Hemispheric Differences Measured in Real-Life Portraits Using Pupil Diameter and Subjective

Aesthetic Preferences," *Experimental Brain Research* 219 (April 2012): 447–55, https://doi.org/10.1007/s00221-012-3091-y.

Elena Mascalzoni, Daniel Osorio, Lucia Regolin, and Giorgio Vallortigara, "Symmetry Perception by Poultry Chicks and Its Implications for Three-Dimensional Object Recognition," *Proceedings of the Royal Society B: Biological Sciences* 279 (2012): 841–46, https://doi.org/10.1098/rspb.2011.1486.

Danette C. Taylor, "How Likely Is Complete Recovery from Bell's Palsy (Idiopathic Facial Paralysis)," *Medscape,* June 14, 2019, https://www.medscape.com/answers/1146903-20225/how-likely-is-complete-recovery-from-bell-palsy-idiopathic-facial-paralysis-ifp.

Arthur Aron, Edward Melinat, Elaine N. Aron, Robert Darrin Vallone, and Renee J. Bator, "The Experimental Generation of Interpersonal Closeness: A Procedure and Some Preliminary Findings," *Personality and Social Psychology Bulletin* 23, no. 4 (April 1997): 363–77, http://stafforini.com/docs/Aron%20et%20al%20-%20The%20experimental%20generation%20of%20interpersonal%20closeness.pdf.

Jessica R. Jackson, William W. Eaton, Nicola G. Cascella, Alessio Fasano, and Deanna L. Kelly, "Neurologic and Psychiatric Manifestations of Celiac Disease and Gluten Sensitivity," *Psychiatric Quarterly* 83 (March 2012): 91–102, https://doi.org/10.1007/s11126-011-9186-y.

L. Fu, C. Bundy, and S. A. Sadiq, "Psychological Distress in People with Disfigurement from Facial Palsy," *Eye* 25 (2011): 1322–26, https://doi.org/10.1038/eye.2011.158.

Geoffrey C. Casazza, Seth R. Schwartz, and Richard K. Gurgel, "Systematic Review of Facial Nerve Outcomes after Middle Fossa Decompression and Transmastoid Decompression for Bell's Palsy with Complete Facial Paralysis," *Otology & Neurotology* 39, no. 10 (December 2018): 1311–18, https://doi.org/10.1097/MAO.0000000000001979.

San-Yeon Lee, Jeon Seong, and Young Ho Kim, "Clinical Implication of Facial Nerve Decompression in Complete Bell's Palsy: A Systemic Review and Meta-Analysis," *Clinical and Experimental Otorhinolaryngology* 12, no. 4 (November 2019): 348–59, http://doi.org/10.21053/ceo.2019.00535.

Marco Iacoboni, *Mirroring People: The Science of Empathy and How We Connect with Others* (New York: Picador, 2008), 134.

About the Author

SARAH RUHL is a playwright, essayist, and poet. Her fifteen plays include *In the Next Room, or the vibrator play*; *The Clean House*; and *Eurydice*. She has been a two-time Pulitzer Prize finalist, a Tony Award nominee, and the recipient of the MacArthur "genius" Fellowship. Her plays have been produced on and off-Broadway, around the country, and internationally, and have been translated into many languages. Her book *100 Essays I Don't Have Time to Write* was a *New York Times* Notable Book. Her other books include *Letters from Max*, with Max Ritvo, and *44 Poems for You*. She has received the Steinberg Playwright Award, the Samuel French Award, the Feminist Press Under 40 Award, the National Theater Conference Person of the Year Award, the Susan Smith Blackburn Prize, a Whiting Award, a Lilly Award, and a PEN/Laura Pels International Foundation for Theater Award for mid-career playwrights. She teaches at the Yale School of Drama, and she lives in Brooklyn with her husband, Tony Charuvastra, a child psychiatrist, and their three children.

www.sarahruhlplaywright.com
Instagram: @sarah_ruhl_